The Catholic Handbook for
Visiting the Sick and Homebound

2008
Year A

LTP

LITURGY
TRAINING
PUBLICATIONS

All explanations of the reading were written by Rev. J K Fuller and originally published in *Daily Prayer 2008* except those found on page 143 (Kathy Hendricks, *At Home with the Word 2005*), pages 149, 150, 161, 171, 190, 209, 212, 217, 219, 228, 229, 230, 233, 242, 243, 252, 253, (Michael Cameron, Dominic Doherty, Fr. Mark Daniel Kirby, Maria Leonard, and Pauline Viviano, *At Home with the Word 2005*), pages 145, 153, 154, 166, 202, 242, (Robert C. Rabe and David Cronan, *Daily Prayer 2007*), and page 204 (Martin Connell, *Workbook for Lectors 2005*).

Nihil Obstat	*Imprimatur*
Reverend Brian J. Fischer, S.T.L.	Reverend John F. Canary, S.T.L., D.Min.
Censor Deputatus	Vicar General
May 30, 2007	Archdiocese of Chicago
	May 31, 2007

Concordat cum originali
Monsignor James P. Moroney
Executive Director
USCCB Secretariat for the Liturgy

Inside art by Sister Mary Grace Thul, OP

LTP appreciates your comments and suggestions. Email us at CHVS@ltp.org.

THE CATHOLIC HANDBOOK FOR VISITING THE SICK AND HOMEBOUND 2008 © 2007 Archdiocese of Chicago: Liturgy Training Publications, 1800 North Hermitage Avenue, Chicago IL 60622; 1-800-933-1800, fax 1-800-933-7094, e-mail orders@ltp.org. All rights reserved. See our Web site at www.LTP.org.

Printed in Canada.

ISBN 978-1-56854-633-9
VS08

TABLE OF CONTENTS

Pastoral Care of the Dying

THE GOSPEL AND EXPLANATION OF THE READING

Advent

Christmas

Ordinary Time I

Lent

Easter

Ordinary Time II

PSALM 23

The Good Shepherd

The Lamb himself will be their shepherd and will lead them to the springs of living waters (Revelation 7:17)

The Lord is my shepherd;
there is nothing I shall want.
Fresh and green are the pastures
where he gives me repose.
Near restful waters he leads me,
to revive my drooping spirit.

He guides me along the right path;
he is true to his name.
If I should walk in the valley of darkness
no evil would I fear.
You are there with your crook and your staff;
with these you give me comfort.

You have prepared a banquet for me
in the sight of my foes.
My head you have anointed with oil;
my cup is overflowing.

Surely goodness and kindness shall follow me
all the days of my life.
In the Lord's own house shall I dwell
for ever and ever.

INTRODUCTION

Come to me, all you who labor and are burdened,
and I will give you rest. Take my yoke upon you and
learn from me, for I am meek and humble of heart;
and you will find rest for yourselves. For my yoke is
easy, and my burden light.

–Matthew 11:28

Suffering wears a thousand faces, and every face is Christ's. When we suffer sickness, loss, or violence, or the harsher effects of aging in ourselves or in those we love, we cannot really understand the reasons, but we can choose the rock on which to stand. We are members of the Body of Christ. Christ our Head becomes present in our suffering; in our dying we share his death; his voyage through death to the glory of the Resurrection becomes our journey. In him, we are held securely in the face of the anxiety, fear, anger, guilt, and grief that sickness, aging, or suffering can bring. In him, we can grow out of the small, even petty, focus on ourselves to which illness tempts us into the greatness of heart which is every Christian's destiny.

But we cannot do it alone. One of the deepest causes of suffering experienced by those whom sickness or aging confines to the narrow world of home, hospital, or geriatric facility is a sense of isolation. We may feel misunderstood, rejected, abandoned by the healthy world of which we were a part, even by those who love us, even by God. There is something wrong with us. We are no longer useful. We cause other people discomfort and inconvenience. We may know how we "ought" to pray in times of suffering, but we can't seem to do it. We can't even go to church.

When we have suffered traumatic loss or violence, we may suffer a similar sense of loneliness. Our experience has set us apart. We may feel that no one can understand what we have endured. We find ourselves unable to take an interest in the world of everyday concerns about which others are busy. We may even find ourselves ill at ease with our ordinary companions in faith and worship. Our usual forms of prayer no longer seem to suffice. We have questions that are difficult to answer: why me? Why has God allowed this to happen? We may be angry with God *and* ashamed of our anger. On the other hand, we may find ourselves more deeply in communion with the suffering Christ or with his bereaved and sorrowful Mother than before yet separated from others by the intensity of our spiritual experience.

Ministers of Care, both the laity and the ordained, are sent to step across the moat that isolates the sufferers, bringing them the comfort of personal presence and prayer. Ministries of care are as diverse as the parishes that sponsor them. Some parishes may have full-time lay pastoral associates or other employees who specialize in pastoral care. These lay people may have been specially trained, participating in pastoral care internships (Clinical Pastoral Education), or receiving undergraduate or graduate degrees in pastoral care or diocesan or national certification. Parishes also may be fortunate to have volunteers who provide pastoral care to those in hospitals, hospices, nursing homes, prisons, police stations, crisis centers, and to those who are dying or have lost a loved one. These volunteers can provide music, proclaim scripture, offer words of consolation and hope, or simply silent presence.

The most familiar ministry of care is that of Extraordinary Minister of Holy Communion. The word *extraordinary* can be confusing. In this case, the Church uses it officially to distinguish between ordained bishops, priests, and deacons, who are the *ordinary* ministers of Holy Communion, and specially commissioned lay people who fill the gaps, so to speak, when there are not enough ordinary ministers to give Holy Communion to everyone at Mass or to take Holy Communion to the sick and the homebound. The words *extraordinary* and *ordinary* as they are used here may strike us as odd because they recall a time when there were so many priests that there was no need for lay people to take on this role.

This handbook is specially designed for the use of *lay* Ministers of Care, so it does *not* contain the rites for the sacraments of Penance or the Anointing of the Sick, or the special prayers and blessings used by ordained bishops, priests, or deacons. All lay ministers who provide care to those who are sick, homebound, isolated, or suffering in some way will benefit from the contents of this book.

You, as a Minister of Care, have been called to be a sign and a bridge. Sent by the parish, you are the living witness that the community of faith and worship has not forgotten the absent sick, the invisible elderly, and the unseen sufferers. Praying with them as a representative of Christ living in the Church, you are a sign that God is and wants to be with them. You draw them back into conscious communion with the whole Body of Christ. They, and in many cases their caregivers, are not alone.

The Church has provided two official books which contain a wealth of rites for those who visit, pray with, and/or bring Holy Communion to the sick, aging, dying, or others who are struggling with addiction, personal violence, or the loss of a child through miscarriage—especially those cut off from fully participating in the liturgical life of their local Church (especially, the Sunday Mass). These ritual books are called *Pastoral Care of the Sick: Rites of Anointing and Viaticum* and the *Book of Blessings. Pastoral Care of the Sick* contains rites specific to those who are sick and dying, providing orders of prayer for the sacraments of the Eucharist, Penance, and Anointing of the Sick. The *Book of Blessings* provides multiple orders of blessing which give God praise for various needs and occasions. What you have in your hand, *The Catholic Handbook for Visiting the Sick and Homebound 2008*, is a booklet containing all of the rituals from *Pastoral Care of the Sick* and the *Book of Blessings* that can be used by lay people when visiting the sick and the homebound. Everything you will need is right here! You will be able to use this book when you are sent to give Holy Communion to other parishioners and/or pray with: those who are confined to their homes, to hospitals, or to geriatric centers; those who have suffered the traumatic loss of a child through miscarriage; those who suffer from addictions; and those who have been victims of violence. The most important resource you have as a minister, though, is your personal relationship with Christ, our healer and our Savior. You too are the face of Christ.

USING THIS BOOK

The Catholic Handbook for Visiting the Sick and Homebound 2008 will tell you what the Church asks of you, as her spokesperson, to say and do when you visit and/or give Holy Communion to those who suffer. You need not worry about making up prayers—here they are! In fact, *except* where the rite itself calls for adaptation, you must use the prayers as they are written because they express the common faith of the Catholic Church to which we all committed ourselves in Baptism. We are called to help one another to grow into the full breadth and depth of that faith. When you pray in the name of the Church you represent, you are asking the sick and others who gather with them to say "Amen," that is, "Yes, I agree, I will abide by that, and I want God to do what you are asking in our name." The Church is very clear that "no one has the authority to add, remove, or change anything in the liturgy" (Constitution on the Sacred Liturgy, #22.2).

THE CONTENTS OF THE BOOK

As a Minister of Care you will be called upon to offer those you visit an opportunity to benefit from the strengthening power of prayer by making use of one of the other services of prayer and blessing provided by the Church. This book contains everything you will need to give Holy Communion as well as additional rites for praying with the sick and others who suffer for various reasons. The rites and prayers are divided into three sections:

- Section 1: Blessings of and Visits to the Sick and Suffering

- Section 2: Holy Communion

- Section 3: Pastoral Care of the Dying

Each of these sections contains the official rites and orders of prayer as provided by the Church in both the *Book of Blessings* and *Pastoral Care of the Sick: Rites of Anointing and Viaticum*. The following notes will help you navigate these rites.

BLESSINGS OF AND VISITS TO THE SICK AND SUFFERING

Visiting and Blessing the Sick: You may be sent to visit the sick simply to pray with them. However, sometimes you may be prepared to give Holy Communion, but you discover that those you are visiting are unable to receive for some reason. At still other times, you may be visiting Catholic patients in an institution, but others who are not Catholic recognize you as a minister and ask you to pray with them. You need not turn away, feeling that you have nothing to offer. These are some of the occasions when you could use these rites for visiting the sick and the suffering—either to prepare them to receive Holy Communion during a later visit or simply to enable them to draw strength and comfort from the healing presence of Christ who has promised to be there whenever two or three gather in his name (see Matthew 18:20).

Titles of these rites: A word about names is needed to prevent confusion. The book entitled *Pastoral Care of the Sick: Rites of Anointing and Viaticum* provides two rites for visiting the sick: "Visits to the Sick" and "Visits to a Sick Child". The former is used with adults. The *Book of Blessings* also provides two rites. However, these rites are entitled "Orders for Blessing the Sick: Order for the Blessing of Adults" and "Order for the Blessing of Children". Here the word "order" simply means "order of service". The two rites from *Pastoral Care of the Sick* are simple prayers for visiting the sick. In this section of the *Catholic Handbook*, "Orders for the Blessing of the Sick" (pages 22–61) are followed by "Visits to the Sick" (pages 62–79).

The Liturgies: The "Orders for the Blessing of the Sick" begin with a simple sign of the cross and invitation to pray followed by a reading of the Word of God whereas "Visits to the Sick" begin with the reading. "Visits to the Sick" continues with the Lord's Prayer and a choice of concluding prayers designed to address some of the different circumstances in which the sick might find themselves. For example, concluding prayer option A references those who "suffer pain, illness or disease"; option B pleas for the sick to be restored to health; and option C requests that the sick may find "peace of mind". Consider your options in relation to the situation of the person you are visiting. If you happen to be visiting someone who isn't Catholic, you may use this order of service, but remember to remind them tactfully that Catholics end the prayer after "deliver us from evil." If not, be prepared for them to add the longer ending, "for thine is the kingdom, the power and the glory" before the "Amen". Above all, you do not want to cause distress to anyone.

In the "Orders for Blessing of the Sick" the Word of God may be followed with an explanation of the reading and then a litany of intercession. The Church urges the minister to encourage the sick to participate in Christ's redemptive work by uniting their sufferings to his and by praying for the needs of the world. Prayer for others is an effective antidote to the self-preoccupation to which sickness and aging can tempt us. Intercessions provide an excellent way of meeting this need. You may allow participants the opportunity to add petitions of their own, but beware of causing embarrassment by prolonging the silence if it becomes clear that they have nothing to say.

Both the rites for "Visits to the Sick" and "Orders for the Blessing of the Sick" end with prayers of blessing which may be said over the person who is ill. The "Orders for the Blessing of the Sick" provides two prayers of blessing. The first option is for several sick people, whereas the second option is for only one sick person. The rite stipulates that the minister is to make the sign of the cross on the forehead of the sick while saying the prayer. The gesture may be unexpected or unfamiliar, especially coming from a lay minister, so it is wise to let people know what you are preparing to do. This may be followed with a prayer for the protection of the Blessed Virgin Mary. The rite suggests singing a familiar Marian song, such as *Hail, Holy Queen*. If music is unavailable, only sing if those you are visiting are able to participate.

"Visits to the Sick" includes two prayers of blessing: one for a sick person and one for the elderly. Please note that the lay minister does not make the same gesture as given in "Orders for the Blessing of the Sick." Simply say the prayer.

"Orders for the Blessing of the Sick" and "Visits to the Sick" end with a concluding prayer. In both rites, the "lay minister invokes the Lord's blessing on the sick and all present by signing himself or herself with the sign of the cross".

The "Order for the Blessing of Children" (page 31) and "Visits to a Sick Child" (page 75) follow the same pattern as those used for adults, but they use simpler language. You will have to decide which rite or order of blessing is appropriate to use with older children. A word of caution: before you make the sign of the cross on the child's head during the blessing, it would be wise to alert parents or caregivers to see if they have any objections. It is also wise to explain this to the child. Remember that very sick children may have experienced unpleasant medical procedures and may fear the unexplained touch of an unfamiliar adult.

Visiting and Blessing those who Suffer: In addition to the rites for visiting and blessing the sick, the *Catholic Handbook* contains three additional services for blessing those who suffer and may not be able to participate in Sunday Eucharist:

- Blessing a Person Suffering from Addiction or from Substance Abuse
- Blessing a Victim of Crime or Oppression
- Blessing Parents after a Miscarriage

If you visit the sick, you may meet people in need of one of these special blessings. You will sometimes meet them in a health care setting. For example, sometimes a patient has been hospitalized as a result of addictive behavior or alcohol and drug abuse. Sometimes you may meet a patient who has suffered personal violence, such as domestic abuse, rape, a drive-by shooting, injuries sustained in an accident caused by a drunk driver, or injuries sustained at the hands of those engaged in criminal activities, such as robbery. Sometimes you may find that a woman has suffered a miscarriage, and she and her husband are grieving together. You may also find people among the families of those you are visiting to pray with them or give them Holy Communion at home or in an institutional environment. An elderly person might indicate a child or grandchild who is suffering one of these needs and ask you to pray with them. You may be among those assigned to special ministries of care in settings such as support groups.

Be aware that the reason for the need may be recent, or long-standing. Sometimes, someone who is coping with illness, confinement in a geriatric facility, or other situation which has brought you to them will want to discuss something that happened long ago and continues to haunt them. Periods of inactivity brought on by sickness or aging give us plenty of time to think and may spur us to make peace with the past in a new way. These orders of blessing offer that opportunity.

Whenever you meet someone in one of these situations, you may use the appropriate order of blessing from the pages that follow. All of them follow the same pattern: an opening rite (sign of the cross, simple greeting, optional introduction), reading and response, including the opportunity to comment on the reading, intercessions, the Lord's Prayer, and a prayer of blessing directed to the particular needs of participants, and a concluding rite (general blessing). The Church encourages adaptation, provided the order of service is followed and the major elements included. For example, you might want to personalize the opening introduction, following the general pattern of the one provided here. Here is one example of a personalized introduction to the Order for Blessing a Victim of Crime or Oppression. Imagine that you are praying with and for a young woman who is a victim of date rape. You might say something like this:

"God has always shown care and compassion for people who have suffered acts of violence, like the one that has brought you here. We commend you, [use the woman's name], to God, who binds up all our wounds, heals us from the pain of betrayal, and restores us to our rightful dignity as a child of God." The introduction now refers to the victim's own experience, uses her name, and avoids language that could summon up frightening images of being held by a male person.

You will want to choose those intercessions that are most appropriate. You may invite participants to add their own and you may do so as well. Turning one's own suffering into prayer for others is both a way of uniting oneself with the redemptive suffering of Christ and turning one's attention outward. If you are accustomed to using the "Orders for Blessing of the Sick", please note that there are some differences between them and these orders of blessing for those otherwise in distress. In particular, these latter orders call for the Lord's Prayer, which often provides the comfort of a familiar prayer; and they do *not* call for the minister to touch the person while saying the prayer of blessing for them. This can be an important courtesy when using this order for blessing with those who have suffered personal violence and shy away from being touched by strangers, even in prayers of blessing.

Like the "Orders for the Blessing of the Sick", these orders also provide a shorter form: a short invitation to prayer, a short reading, and a prayer of blessing. These short forms are particularly useful when ministering to those who have very recently experienced a crisis in addiction, an incident of violence, or a miscarriage, and are too distressed to concentrate on a longer ritual. They are also helpful when you are visiting the person for some other reason and find a need to help them deal with one of these issues.

One of the hidden benefits of the Church's rites of prayer is that they teach us to think in harmony with the Church. If you have never experienced the particular need for which you are blessing someone, your good intentions may sometimes stumble in trying to find the right words of comfort. It is easy to offend without meaning to by offering what sound like platitudes to those who are in the immediate throes of suffering. It is also easy to give impressions of God that hurt rather than help them. The texts of these rites will assist you to reflect on how to focus your comments. They are also impersonal enough that they offer room for participants in the rites to take them as words from God to be pondered and applied to their own experience rather than as personal remarks about their own faith response to what they have suffered.

On a practical note, all of the orders recommend an opening and closing song. If they are celebrated in a public setting, with advanced preparation, music may be an effective option because it engages the human spirit so deeply and speaks so strongly at a level beyond words. However, if you are visiting alone, you may or may not be able to supply this element, and participants may or may not be able join in. Encourage liturgical musicians to join the minister of care. Find out if the place you are going to has music resources, or if you will need to bring worship aids, song books, or hymnals.

HOLY COMMUNION

This book provides two rites for lay ministers to give Holy Communion to the sick: "Communion in Ordinary Circumstances" and "Communion in a Hospital or Institution".

Communion in Ordinary Circumstances: The first form, called "Communion in Ordinary Circumstances", is especially useful if you are taking Holy Communion to the sick or aging in their homes. It assumes two things: first, that you have enough time to lead the full rite of Holy Communion including a short Liturgy of the Word; second, that those you visit are well enough to participate in a full service. The Church urges us always to consider the needs of the sick or aging. If they are very weak or tire quickly, it's better to shorten or omit elements like the explanation after the reading or the General Intercessions (Prayer of the Faithful), or simply to use the shorter form called "Communion in a Hospital or Institution" even in a home setting.

Communion in a Hospital or Institution: This second form, "Communion in a Hospital or Institution", provides a minimal format mainly intended for use when you are visiting many patients individually in an institutional setting. The Church expresses a strong preference for avoiding this abbreviated format even in an institution. Instead, it is suggested that, if possible, you gather several residents together in one or more areas and celebrate the full rite of "Communion in Ordinary Circumstances". If that is not possible, the Church recommends that you add elements from the fuller rite, such as the reading of the word, unless participants are too weak. On the other hand, in the case of extremely sick people, you may shorten even the rite for Communion in a Hospital or Institution by omitting as much of the rite as necessary. Try to include at least a greeting, the Lord's Prayer, the customary responses that precede Holy Communion itself, and the closing prayer.

PASTORAL CARE OF THE DYING

Viaticum: Holy Communion for the Dying: Any of the seriously ill, but especially hospice patients, may move more quickly than expected toward death. A person who faces death within days should receive Holy Communion under the form of Viaticum. "Viaticum" means something like "travel with you," but it is often translated as food for the journey. Although the sacrament of the Anointing of the Sick strengthens us in the face of sickness, the Eucharist as Viaticum is the sacrament that, together with Penance, prepares a person for the final journey through death to everlasting life in Christ. Catholics are obligated to receive Viaticum if possible. The sacrament of the Anointing of the Sick may be given after Penance but *before* Viaticum. If the person is unable to swallow, they may receive the Sacrament of Penance *instead* of Viaticum; however, the Church teaches that Viaticum is the essential sacrament when we are in the face of death. The time for using the special comforting and strengthening prayers of the Rite of Viaticum to administer Holy Communion is while the person is still conscious and able to swallow. Once death has become imminent, dying persons may receive Viaticum every day for as long as they are able. An Extraordinary Minister of Holy Communion may and should give Viaticum to the dying. If the dying person has not received sacramental absolution, please make sure the person has the opportunity for both the Sacrament of Penance and, if desired, Anointing of the Sick.

Commendation for the Dying and Prayers for the Dead: While the sacraments, especially Viaticum, unite the dying with Christ in his passage from this life to the next, we also gather with the dying and those around them to sustain this union through the prayer and faith of the Church.

"Commendation for the Dying" does not follow a fixed pattern. You may select any texts from the prayers, litanies, aspirations, psalms and readings, or you may use other familiar prayers, such as the rosary. If you have had the opportunity to talk with the dying person and loved ones or others present, choose texts you think will sustain and strengthen them according to their spiritual needs and other circumstances. Pray the texts slowly and quietly, allowing ample opportunities for silence. You may repeat them as often as needed, especially prayers that have special meaning for those present. Even the dying who are unconscious can sometimes hear more than we realize. If the dying cannot hear, loved ones present will find comfort in the prayers.

If you minister in an institutional setting, you may find that those who are not Catholic will ask you to pray with and for them. You may use these texts with and for any who are in need of the consolation of prayer. The texts drawn from the Bible are especially likely to bring comfort.

Once death has occurred, you will find both prayers for the dead and prayers for family and friends on pp. 134, "Prayers for the Dead".

Ritual Preparation: All of the rites are simple to follow. Look them over before making your visits in order to familiarize yourself with the order of prayer. Directions are included and parts are clearly marked so that you can easily lead the communicants in prayer. The texts of the rites included in this book are specifically for lay ministers.

THE GOSPEL FOR SUNDAYS AND HOLY DAYS OF OBLIGATION

Following the rites are the Gospel readings for Sundays and holy days of obligation for Year A. Remember the Church is on a three year cycle of readings. In 2009 the readings will be from Year B. The Church recommends reading the week's Sunday Gospel during the Communion rite as one important way of uniting the communicants in spirit with the parish from which sickness or age has separated them.

In this book, the Gospel is clearly labeled by date and the title of particular observances so that you can easily find the appropriate reading. For example, if you make your visit during the Second Week of Ordinary Time, you will use the Gospel for the Second Sunday of Ordinary Time. In 2008, this Sunday of Ordinary Time is January 20. Simply look for the date and the title of the celebration and you will know which Gospel to use. These are also indicated in the table of contents of this book. For some observances, such as Palm Sunday, the Lectionary provides a longer and shorter form of the Gospel. For simplicity, only the shorter form is included in this resource.

If you are visiting on a holy day of obligation, use the Gospel prescribed for these days. You can also locate the Gospel for holy days of obligation by date and title. In the dioceses of the United States of America, the holy days of obligation occurring in 2008 are:

- Solemnity of the Immaculate Conception of the Blessed Virgin Mary (December 8, 2007)

- Solemnity of the Nativity of the Lord (December 25, 2007)

- Solemnity of the Blessed Virgin Mary, the Mother of God (January 1, 2008)

- Solemnity of the Ascension of the Lord (May 1 or May 4, 2008)

- Solemnity of the Assumption of the Blessed Virgin Mary (August 15, 2008)

"Regarding the Ascension of the Lord, the ecclesiastical Provinces [dioceses] of Boston, Hartford, New York, Newark, Philadelphia, and the state of Nebraska have retained its proper celebration on the proper Thursday [May 1, 2008]. In these Provinces [dioceses], the readings for the day are from the solemnity of the Ascension of the Lord. In all other Provinces [dioceses] that have transferred this solemnity to the Seventh Sunday of Easter, on that day (7th Sunday of Easter), the readings are from the Ascension of the Lord" (http://www.usccb.org/norms/1246.htm).

Please also note that the solemnity of All Saints on November 1 is *not* a holy day of obligation in 2008 because it falls on a Saturday.

If you are visiting very young sick children, you might want to obtain a copy of the appropriate reading from the *Lectionary for Masses with Children* from your parish. Another option is to read the Gospel(s) recommended in "Visits to a Sick Child".

If you are praying with those who are struggling with addictions or the aftermath of violence or with parents who have suffered the loss of a child through miscarriage, you will usually find the readings recommended in the orders of blessing more appropriate to their circumstances than the Gospel for the Sunday. However, if appropriate, feel free to use the Gospels for Sundays and holy days of obligation. To discern which readings to use, it is best to look over the order of service *before* the visit occurs.

EXPLANATION OF THE READINGS

You will notice that the rites offer an opportunity for the Minister of Care to give a brief explanation of the reading with special reference to the experience of those with whom you are praying and, where appropriate, of their caregivers. If you are using the Sunday or holy day reading, you might want to base your explanation and reflection on the parish Sunday homily in order to deepen the sense of connection you are trying encourage. If you feel uncomfortable about speaking, you will find a brief explanation of the reading after each Sunday and holy day Gospel reading. If you choose to read it from the book, it would be a good idea to ponder it and make it your own so that the words come from your heart and not merely from the page. The Word of God itself creates a bond between reader and hearers, breaking down the sense of isolation that afflicts sufferers. Explanatory words that are spoken, or even read, with sincerity and personal conviction will support this pastoral relationship more effectively than words read mechanically.

PATRON SAINTS

Finally, there is a list of saints who the Church has identified as particular intercessors, companions, and guides for those suffering various kinds of afflictions, whether physical or emotional. If you feel that those with whom you pray would welcome the company and support of a saint, you might want to include the saint's name in the intercessions (petitions) and suggest that those you are visiting continue to ask for the saint's help. An example of an intercession is:

For all those who suffer from throat cancer, especially N. (insert the name of the person or persons present), that through the intercession of Saint Blaise, may find comfort and strength, we pray to the Lord.

This book does not provide any information about the saints listed, but there are many books and Web sites where you can find their stories. Such resources are *Butler's Lives of the Saints* (published by the Liturgical Press) and Catholic Online (www.catholic.org/saints).

BEYOND THE BOOK

The official rites offer appropriate prayers and clear directions, but they don't tell you everything you need to know in order to lead the rituals effectively. Here are some practical hints that may help.

GETTING FROM THE PARISH CHURCH TO YOUR PASTORAL ASSIGNMENT

Scheduling a Visit: Some parishes assign ministers to visit particular people but encourage them to make their own arrangements regarding the day and time. Both those in need of your ministry and their families or caregivers, at home or in institutional facilities, appreciate being able to negotiate appropriate times for a pastoral visit or Holy Communion. It gives them an opportunity to make sure that they and those they would like to have present can be there. For example, if you're visiting the sick, you don't want to drop in when patients are absent from their rooms for tests or treatments.

If you are asked to take Holy Communion to the sick and the home-bound at times other than during Sunday Mass, please make sure your training includes information about where to find the tabernacle key and how to approach the tabernacle reverently, open it, and transfer the hosts you will need from the ciborium in which they are kept to the container you will use to carry the Blessed Sacrament to the sick (see below). It is particularly important to arrange with the parish coordinator a convenient time for you to obtain the tabernacle key, because it is not permitted to keep the Eucharist at home or carry it all day as you go about your ordinary business before visiting communicants.

Ordinarily, when taking the Blessed Sacrament from the tabernacle, you would pray briefly before the tabernacle, wash your fingers in a small vessel of water that is usually kept beside the tabernacle for that purpose, wipe them on a finger towel also usually kept there, and genuflect after opening the tabernacle. If your parish does not provide either the small vessel or finger towel, wash your hands in the sacristy or otherwise clean your fingers as best you are able over the sacrarium. If you have unused hosts left over at the end of your rounds, you must bring them back to the parish church and replace them in the tabernacle. After closing the tabernacle, you again wash your fingers. You may also cleanse the empty pyx in the sacrarium if it appears to contain crumbs.

Fill it with water, drink the water, and dry the pyx carefully on a finger towel, if available. If you wish to avoid having hosts that must be returned, you can give the last few communicants more than one host so that all the hosts are consumed or consume them yourself as part of the communion rite during your last visit, provided all the usual requirements for communion are met. However, you may not simply consume them yourself after your last visit because Holy Communion is always received in the context of public prayer rather than simply as a matter of convenience by the minister alone. Similarly, you may not take the remaining hosts home to return later to the Church because the Eucharist must be kept in a tabernacle or other designated locked place of reservation in a church.

Bringing What You Need: Make a checklist of what you want to have with you before you leave home. You'll find some suggestions below. Don't forget this book! It does happen. If it does, don't panic, and don't fail to keep your appointment. As a precaution, make every effort to memorize the outline of the rites you expect to use or keep a copy of a simple outline in your pocket, wallet, or purse. In this case, do make up your own prayer, but keep it very short and simple. Borrow a Bible or summarize the Gospel in your own words. God works through all our weaknesses and mistakes.

Carrying the Blessed Sacrament: The Blessed Sacrament is carried in a small container called a *pyx* or in another dignified vessel reserved exclusively for that purpose. Your parish will probably supply you with what you need. Some pyxes can be worn or carried in a pouch on a cord around the neck. When you are carrying the Blessed Sacrament, remember and attend reverently to Christ, choosing your activities appropriately, without becoming artificially silent or stilted in your conversation, especially with those who are not aware of what you are carrying or of its significance. On the one hand, avoid distractions such as loud music, "talk" programs or other television shows, movies or DVDs/tapes, or other things that would disturb prayer while you are en route. On the other hand, while avoiding such distractions, be careful not to be rude to people who greet you or speak to you in passing as you walk to your destination. Christ is not offended by the company and conversation of human beings! You should make your Communion visit immediately upon leaving the Church.

PREPARING AN ENVIRONMENT FOR PRAYER

ENCOUNTERING CHRIST IN PERSONS

Church ministry is always personal. It is important that you spend a few minutes at the beginning of your visit to get to know those present and give them a chance to feel comfortable with you. Your parish may be able to supply you with helpful information in advance of your visit. In return, it would be useful to other Ministers of Care if you were to report back what you had learned about the condition, circumstances, and needs of those you visit.

When you arrive, put those present at ease by engaging in a few moments of personal conversation. Tell them your name and remind them that the parish has sent you. Ask how they are and listen attentively to their answers. If you are visiting the sick, show your interest and concern, but remember that you are not there to offer medical advice or to pass judgment on medical matters, even if you yourself are a professional medical caregiver. If you can, address those you are visiting by name, but be aware that not everyone likes to be addressed by a first name without permission. Sickness, debilitating aging, and other forms of public suffering often rob people of their sense of personal dignity, so treating people with respect is an important dimension of your ministry. Whatever their condition, you and they are both collaborators in Christ's work. Ministry is a two-way street: those whom you visit are serving you by their witness to Christ suffering as much as you are serving them by offering them Christ's loving comfort. Take note of any special needs you see: is the sufferer low on energy, in pain, limited in motion, hard of hearing, angry, sad, or seemingly depressed? You will want to tailor the length, content, and style of the celebration accordingly.

CREATING AN ENVIRONMENT FOR PRAYER

PREPARING YOURSELF TO LEAD PRAYER

The world of the suffering, especially those confined to home or, even more so, to a hospital or geriatric facility may not feel much like a place of prayer. The most important element in creating an environment for prayer is you. The minister who prays while leading others in prayer is the most powerful invitation one can offer to those who need to be called from all the preoccupations of suffering into deeper awareness of the mystery of God present and acting in our midst.

Here are some steps you can take to develop this important skill:

1) Devote time for praying, reading, and meditating on the texts of the prayers and readings provided in this book. You will best pray them in public if you have already prayed them many times in private.

2) Familiarize yourself thoroughly with the structure and flow of the rites so that you can concentrate on the people rather than the book. You need not memorize prayers or readings. Simply know what comes next and where to find it.

3) Before you go into the building or room, pray briefly, asking Christ to work through you; after the visit, pause to give thanks.

4) Reflect on your experience after you return home. Were there moments during the celebration when you felt uncertain or distracted? Why? What could you do next time to make yourself more at ease so that you can pray more attentively without losing contact with those you are leading in prayer? Sharing experience with other Ministers of Care and/or parish staff can be a useful way to continue and deepen everyone's on-going ministry formation.

PREPARING THE ROOM FOR PRAYER

You can also take some simple steps to establish an atmosphere that encourages prayer when circumstances allow. A small standing crucifix, cross, or icon heightens consciousness of Christ. Appropriate lighting can help, where possible. In an institutional setting, for example, a lamp or sunlight creates a more humane environment than do fluorescent lights. If you are taking Holy Communion to someone, take a small white cloth and a candle with you to prepare a place on which to put the pyx containing the Blessed Sacrament as a focus for the celebration as you lead the other prayers. (Be sure you have something with which to light the candle!) A corporal is not required, but if it is used, it is traditionally placed on top of another white cloth rather than on a bare surface. Caregivers familiar with the rite may have prepared a place in advance, but many will not.

Be aware of the restrictions you may face in a health care or geriatric facility. The Communion rite recommends that the minister be accompanied by a candle-bearer and place a candle on the table where the Blessed Sacrament will stand during the celebration, as described above. However, safety regulations usually forbid the use of open flames in institutions. Oxygen and other substances that might be in use are highly flammable. Moreover, you may not be able to find any appropriate surface other than a bedside table or night stand that will have to be cleared before you can set up a place for the Blessed Sacrament. Be prepared to make whatever practical adjustments the circumstances require. If you have never visited a particular hospital unit or nursing home, see if you can find another minister who has and find out what to expect.

PREPARING PARTICIPANTS FOR PRAYER

After a few moments of conversation, find a graceful way to end the social part of the visit without seeming uninterested or abrupt. Then give the participants a simple, brief overview of the rite you will be using so they will know what to expect, unless you know they are already familiar with the rite. Surprises tend to disrupt prayer! It's especially important to decide in advance who will do the reading. The directions say that the reading may be done "by one of those present or by the minister". If you don't know the participants, the best solution might be to ask for a volunteer (and allow the volunteer a few moments to prepare), but remember that not everyone is willing or able to read in public with short notice, especially in times of distress. Finally, mark the beginning of prayer clearly by inviting silent attentiveness, making the sign of the cross and moving into the service itself.

RECOGNIZING THE RECIPIENT

You are ministering not only to those to whom the ritual is addressed but also to those around them, whether loved ones or caregivers. Be sure to include them by looking and speaking to them, as well as to the person who is your focus. When you are saying prayers of blessing over the sufferer, your attention is on that person alone, but all present are invited to join in the "Amen" that affirms and concludes the prayer. Practice with another minister until you can say prayers in such a way that others know when and how to respond without having a book in front of them.

WHO MAY RECEIVE HOLY COMMUNION

Catholic shut-ins, caregivers, or others who assemble with them may receive Holy Communion provided the usual conditions have been met. You can offer that invitation before you begin the Communion rite, being careful not to embarrass or offend those who are not eligible to receive. "The elderly, the infirm and those who care for them can receive the Holy Eucharist even if they have eaten something within the preceding hour" (Code of Canon Law,919 §2).

SPECIAL CIRCUMSTANCES

Unfortunately, neither sickness nor the deterioration sometimes brought on by aging is neat or predictable. The physical, psychological, and spiritual condition of those you visit may have changed since the arrangements for your visit were made. You may need to make unprepared changes in the rite or blessing you are using to meet the current need.

Special Circumstances for Extraordinary Ministers of Holy Communion: If you are taking Holy Communion to the sick or elderly, sometimes those you are visiting will express reluctance to receive. They may or may not want to tell you why. They might be embarrassed to say that they are too nauseated; they might feel alienated from God; they might need sacramental absolution but don't want to say so. You are obviously a person of generosity and compassion, or you wouldn't have volunteered to be an Extraordinary Minister of Holy Communion. However, a Holy Communion visit is not ordinarily the best time to identify and try to resolve serious personal or spiritual problems. Be aware of your status and of the vulnerability of the suffering: you represent the Church, and you have more power than you may realize to make others feel guilty by showing that you disapprove of their decision not to receive Holy Communion or by giving the impression that they have wasted your time. Remember that they are not rejecting you as a person. Rather, they are struggling with something deeper. Offer to pray with them, using the rites provided for visiting or blessing the sick. Invite them to enter more deeply into communion with the suffering and risen Christ who loves them. Let them know what pastoral resources are available to them: offer to return or to send another minister at a more convenient time; provide the parish phone number; offer to let the pastoral staff know that they would like a priest to visit, without forcing them to reply. If the parish distributes a bulletin during the weekend Masses, bring one along to leave with the person to whom you are visiting.

Sometimes you may find that those you are visiting are unable to swallow easily. Consult medical caregivers. If they give permission, you may break the host into the smallest of pieces, place a piece on the person's tongue to dissolve, and follow with a glass of water to make swallowing possible. Be careful with crumbs when you break the host. The best thing to do is to break the host carefully over the pyx so that crumbs will fall into the pyx. If any crumbs fall on the cloth or table on which the pyx has been placed, moisten your finger, pick up all the crumbs very carefully, and consume them reverently.

You may even find that someone cannot ingest the host at all. In such cases, the person may receive the Blood of Christ, but that requires specialized vessels and procedures. Report the circumstances to your pastor, parish coordinator, or to the facility chaplain's office if the person is in a health care or geriatric facility. They will be able to appropriately give Holy Communion. In the meantime, use one of the rites for visiting or blessing the sick to give them the support of your presence and prayer.

Be aware that the hospitalized may not be permitted to take anything by mouth for a period of time prior to certain tests or treatments. Even a small piece of the host received at such times may cause medical personnel to cancel the planned procedure. If you see a sign that says "Nothing by mouth" or "NPO," initials for the Latin phrase (*nil per os*) meaning the same thing, ask a member of the medical staff if you may administer Holy Communion, but expect a "no". In this case, too, you should still pray with the sick or aging, using one of the rites for visiting or blessing the sick. Remember that you still offer them the comfort of Christ's presence in his word and through your own presence and that of the parish you represent.

It is important that the Extraordinary Minister of Holy Communion keeps in mind the sacramental rites which are an essential part of the Church's ministry to the sick and dying and which can be administered *only* by an ordained bishop or priest—the sacraments of Penance (Reconciliation) and the Anointing of the Sick. As appropriate, it is part of your ministry to bring these to the attention of the sick and those confined to their homes, and if needed, to help them contact a priest.

SERVICE TO THE PEOPLE OF GOD

Among these nuts and bolts of the ministry of care, never lose sight of your purpose. You have been commissioned in the name of Christ and his Church to serve as a bridge builder across the isolation that separates the sick and suffering from the parish community of faith and worship. Your deepest task is to carry the good news of the Gospel to those who stand in need of its healing power. With your parish or diocesan training program, the support of your parish pastoral staff and other Ministers of Care, this book and your growing experience, you have many of the tools you will need. However, the most important tool is one that only Christ can provide for you. The more deeply you yourself enter into the heart of the Gospel message, the more clearly you will see that sick and healthy, young and old, grieving and rejoicing, struggling and at peace, are all one Body. In that Body, we are *all* servants at the good news we proclaim, building one another up in faith and love until that day when, by God's gracious gift, we will all dwell together in the Lord's own house for ever and ever.

Genevieve Glen, OSB
Abbey of Saint Walburga
Virginia Dale CO
Revised January 2007

Author Information:
Sister Genevieve Glen, OSB, is a Benedictine nun of the contemplative Abbey of St. Walburga in Virginia Dale, CO. She holds master's degrees in systematic theology from Saint John's University, Collegeville, MN and in spirituality from the Catholic University of America in Washington DC, where she also did extensive doctoral studies in liturgy. She has lectured and written extensively on the Church's rites for the sick and dying. She is co-author of the *Handbook for Ministers of Care*, 2nd edition (Liturgy Training Publications) and contributing editor of *Recovering the Riches of Anointing: A Study of the Sacrament of the Sick* (The Liturgical Press).

THE RITES

Orders for the Blessing of the Sick

INTRODUCTION

376   The blessing of the sick by the ministers of the Church is a very ancient custom, having its origins in the practice of Christ himself and his apostles. When ministers visit those who are sick, they are to respect the provisions of *Pastoral Care of the Sick: Rites of Anointing and Viaticum,* nos. 42–56, but the primary concern of every minister should be to show the sick how much Christ and his Church are concerned for them.

377   The text of *Pastoral Care of the Sick* indicates many occasions for blessing the sick and provides the blessing for formularies.[13]

378   The present order may be used by a priest or deacon. It may also be used by a layperson, who follows the rites and prayers designated for a lay minister. While maintaining the structure and chief elements of the rite, the minister should adapt the celebration to the circumstances of the place and the people involved.

379   When just one sick person is to be blessed, a priest or deacon may use the short formulary given in no. 406.

---

13. See Roman Ritual, *Pastoral Care of the Sick: Rites of Anointing and Viaticum,* no. 54.

ORDER OF BLESSING

A. ORDER FOR THE BLESSING OF ADULTS

INTRODUCTORY RITES

380   *When the community has gathered, the minister says:*

In the name of the Father, and of the Son, and of the Holy Spirit.

All make the sign of the cross and reply:

Amen.

382   *A lay minister greets those present in the following words.*

Brothers and sisters, let us bless the Lord, who went about doing good and healing the sick. Blessed be God now and for ever.
R. *Blessed be God now and for ever.*

Or:

R. *Amen.*

383   *In the following or similar words, the minister prepares the sick and all present for the blessing.*

The Lord Jesus, who went about doing good works and healing sickness and infirmity of every kind, commanded his disciples to care for the sick, to pray for them, and to lay hands on them. In this celebration we shall entrust our sick brothers and sisters to the care of the Lord, asking that he will enable them to bear their pain and suffering in the knowledge that, if they accept their share in the pain of his own passion, they will also share in its power to give comfort and strength.

READING OF THE WORD OF GOD

384   A reader, another person present, or the minister reads a text of sacred Scripture, taken preferably from the texts given in Pastoral Care of the Sick *and the* Lectionary for Mass.[14] *The readings chosen should be those that best apply to the physical and spiritual condition of those who are sick.*

Brothers and Sisters, listen to the words of the second letter of Paul to the Corinthians: 1:3–7

The God of all consolation.

Blessed be the God and Father of our Lord Jesus Christ, the Father of compassion and God of all encouragement, who encourages us in our every affliction, so that we may be able to encourage those who are in any affliction with the encouragement with which we ourselves are encouraged by God. For as Christ's sufferings overflow to us, so through Christ does our encouragement also overflow. If we are afflicted, it is for your encouragement and salvation; if we are encouraged, it is for your encouragement, which enables you to endure the same sufferings that we suffer. Our hope for you is firm, for we know that as you share in the sufferings, you also share in the encouragement.

---

14. See ibid, no. 297; Lectionary for Mass (2nd ed., 1981), nos. 790–795, 796–800 (Ritual Masses: V. Pastoral Care of the Sick and the Dying, 1. Anointing of the Sick and 2. Viaticum), and nos. 933–937 (Masses for Various Needs and Occasions, III. For Various Public Needs, 24. For the Sick).

385   *Or:*

Brothers and sisters, listen to the words of the holy gospel according to Matthew: 11:28–30

Come to me and I will refresh you.

Jesus said to the crowds: "Come to me, all you who labor and are burdened, and I will give you rest. Take my yoke upon you and learn from me, for I am meek and humble of heart; and you will find rest for yourselves. For my yoke is easy, and my burden light."

386   *Or:*

Brothers and sisters, listen to the words of the holy gospel according to Mark: 6:53–56

They laid the sick in the marketplace

After making the crossing, Jesus and his disciples came to land at Gennesaret and tied up there. As they were leaving the boat, people immediately recognized him. They scurried about the surrounding country and began to bring in the sick on mats to wherever they heard he was. Whatever villages or towns or countryside he entered, they laid the sick in the marketplaces and begged him that they might touch only the tassel on his cloak; and as many as touched it were healed.

387   *As circumstances suggest, one of the following responsorial psalms may be sung or said, or some other suitable song.*

R. *Lord, you have preserved my life from destruction.*

Isaiah 38

Once I said,
"In the noontime of life I must depart!
To the gates of the nether world I shall
be consigned
for the rest of my years." *R.*

I said, "I shall see the LORD no more
in the land of the living.
No longer shall I behold my fellow men
among those who dwell in the world." *R.*

My dwelling, like a shepherd's tent,
is struck down and borne away from me;
You have folded up my life, like a weaver
who severs the last thread. *R.*

Those live whom the LORD protects;
yours . . . the life of my spirit.
You have given me health and life. *R.*

Psalm 102:2–3, 24–25
*R. (v. 2) O Lord, hear my prayer, and let my cry come
to you.*

388   *As circumstances suggest, the minister may give those present a brief
explanation of the biblical text, so that they may understand through faith the
meaning of the celebration.*

INTERCESSIONS

389   *The intercessions are then said. The minister introduces them and an assisting minister or one of those present announces the intentions. From the following intentions those best suited to the occasion may be used or adapted, or other intentions that apply to those who are sick and to the particular circumstances may be composed.*

The minister says:

The Lord Jesus loves our brothers and sisters who are ill. With trust let us pray to him that he will comfort them with his grace, saying:
R. *Lord, give those who are sick the comfort of your presence.*

Assisting minister:

Lord Jesus, you came as healer of body and of spirit, in order to cure all our ills. R.

Assisting minister:

You were a man of suffering, but it was our infirmities that you bore, our sufferings that you endured. R.

Assisting minister:

You chose to be like us in all things, in order to assure us of your compassion. R.

Assisting minister:

You experienced the weakness of the flesh in order to deliver us from evil. R.

Assisting minister:

At the foot of the cross your Mother stood as companion in your sufferings, and in your tender care you gave her to us as our Mother. R.

It is your wish that in our own flesh we should fill up what is wanting in your sufferings for the sake of your Body, the Church. *R.*

390   *Instead of the intercessions or in addition to them, one of the following litanies taken from* Pastoral Care of the Sick, *nos. 245 and 138 may be used.*

Minister:

You bore our weakness and carried our sorrows: Lord, have mercy.
R. Lord, have mercy.

Minister:

You felt compassion for the crowd, and went about doing good and healing the sick: Christ, have mercy.
R. Christ, have mercy.

Minister:

You commanded your apostles to lay their hands on the sick in your name: Lord, have mercy.
R. Lord, have mercy.

391   *Or:*

The minister says:

Let us pray to God for our brothers and sisters and for all those who devote themselves to caring for them.

Assisting minister:

Bless *N.* and *N.* and fill them with new hope and strength: Lord, have mercy.
R. Lord, have mercy.

Assisting minister:

Relieve their pain: Lord, have mercy. **R.**

Assisting minister:

Free them from sin and do not let them give way to temptation: Lord, have mercy. **R.**

Assisting minister:

Sustain all the sick with your power: Lord, have mercy. **R.**

Assisting minister:

Assist all who care for the sick: Lord, have mercy. **R.**

Assisting minister:

Give life and health to our brothers and sisters on whom we lay our hands in your name: Lord, have mercy. **R.**

PRAYER OF BLESSING

394   *A lay minister traces the sign of the cross on the forehead of each sick person and says the following prayer of blessing.*

Lord, our God,
who watch over your creatures with unfailing care,
keep us in the safe embrace of your love.
With your strong right hand raise up your servants
      (**N.** and **N.**)
and give them the strength of your own power.

Minister to them and heal their illnesses,
so that they may have from you the help they
    long for.

We ask this through Christ our Lord.
R. Amen.

395   *Or, for one sick person:*
Lord and Father, almighty and eternal God,
by your blessing you give us strength and support
    in our frailty:
turn with kindness toward this your servant N.
Free him/her from all illness and restore him/her
    to health,
so that in the sure knowledge of your goodness
he/she will gratefully bless your holy name.

We ask this through Christ our Lord.
R. Amen.

396   *After the prayer of blessing the minister invites all present to pray*
for the protection of the Blessed Virgin. They may do so by singing or reciting
a Marian antiphon, for example, We turn to you for protection (Sub tuuam
praesidium) *or* Hail, Holy Queen.

CONCLUDING RITE

398   *A lay minister invokes the Lord's blessing on the sick and all present by*
signing himself or herself with the sign of the cross and saying:
May the Lord Jesus Christ,
who went about doing good and healing the sick,

grant that we may have good health
and be enriched by his blessings.
R. Amen.

B. ORDER FOR THE BLESSING OF CHILDREN

*399   For the blessing of sick children, the texts already given are to be adapted
to the children's level, but special intercessions are provided here and a special
prayer of blessing.*

INTERCESSIONS

*400   To the following intentions others may be added that apply to the
condition of the sick children and to the particular circumstances.*

The minister says:

The Lord Jesus loved and cherished the little ones
with a special love. Let us, then, pray to him for
these sick children, saying:
R. *Lord, keep them in all their ways.*

Or:

R. *Lord, hear our prayer.*

Assisting minister:

Lord Jesus, you called the little children to come to
you and said that the kingdom of heaven belongs to
such as these; listen with mercy to our prayers for
these children. (For this we pray:) R.

Assisting minister:

You revealed the mysteries of the kingdom of
heaven, not to the wise of this world, but to little

children; give these children the proof of your love.
(For this we pray:) **R.**

You praised the children who cried out their
Hosannas on the eve of your passion; strengthen
these children and their parents with your holy
comfort. (For this we pray:) **R.**

Assisting minister:
You charged your disciples to take care of the sick;
stand at the side of all those who so gladly devote
themselves to restoring the health of these children.
(For this we pray:) **R.**

PRAYER OF BLESSING

402   *A lay minister, and particularly a mother or father when blessing a sick child, traces the sign of the cross on each child's forehead and then says the following prayer of blessing.*

Father of mercy and God of all consolation,
you show tender care for all your creatures
and give health of soul and body.
Raise up these children
      (*or* this child *or* the son/daughter you have
         given us)
      from their (his/her) sickness.
Then, growing in wisdom and grace in your sight
      and ours,
they (he/she) will serve you all the days of their
      (his/her) life

in uprightness and holiness
and offer the thanksgiving due to your mercy.

We ask this through Christ our Lord.
R. Amen.

C. SHORTER RITE

403   The minister says:
Our help is in the name of the Lord.

All reply:
Who made heaven and earth.

404   One of those present or the minister reads a text of sacred Scripture,
for example:

2 Corinthians 1:3–4
Blessed be the God and Father of our Lord Jesus
Christ, the Father of compassion and God of all
encouragement, who encourages us in our every
affliction, so that we may be able to encourage those
who are in any affliction with the encouragement
with which we ourselves are encouraged by God.

Matthew 11:28–29
Jesus said, "Come to me, all you who labor and
are burdened, and I will give you rest. Take my
yoke upon you and learn from me, for I am meek
and humble of heart; and you will find rest for
yourselves."

As circumstances suggest . . . a lay minister may trace the sign of the cross on the sick person's forehead while saying the prayer.

Lord and Father, almighty and eternal God,
by your blessing you give us strength and support in
      our frailty:
turn with kindness toward your servant, N.
Free him/her from all illness and restore him/her
      to health,
so that in the sure knowledge of your goodness
he/she will gratefully bless your holy name.

We ask this through Christ our Lord.
R. Amen.

Order for the Blessing of a Person Suffering from Addiction or from Substance Abuse

INTRODUCTION

407   Addiction to alcohol, drugs, and other controlled substances causes great disruption in the life of an individual and his or her family. This blessing is intended to strengthen the addicted person in the struggle to overcome addiction and also to assist his or her family and friends.

408   This blessing may also be used for individuals who, although not addicted, abuse alcohol or drugs and wish the assistance of God's blessing in their struggle.

409   Ministers should be aware of the spiritual needs of a person suffering from addiction or substance abuse, and to this end the pastoral guidance on the care of the sick and rites of *Pastoral Care of the Sick* will be helpful.

410   If the recovery process is slow or is marked by relapses, the blessing may be repeated when pastorally appropriate.

411   These orders may be used by a priest or a deacon, and also by a lay person, who follows the rites and prayers designated for a lay minister.

A. ORDER OF BLESSING

INTRODUCTORY RITES

412   When the community has gathered, a suitable song may be sung. After the singing the minister says:

In the name of the Father, and of the Son, and of the Holy Spirit.

All make the sign of the cross and reply:

Amen.

414   A lay minister greets those present in the following words:

Let us praise God our creator, who gives us courage and strength, now and for ever.

R. Amen.

415   In the following or similar words, the minister prepares those present for the blessing.

God created the world and all things in it and entrusted them into our hands that we might use them for our good and for the building up of the Church and human society. Today we pray for N., that God may strengthen him/her in his/her weakness and restore him/her to the freedom of God's children. We pray also for ourselves that we may encourage and support him/her in the days ahead.

READING OF THE WORD OF GOD

416   A reader, another person present, or the minister reads a text of sacred Scripture.

Brothers and sisters, listen to the words of the second letter of Paul to the Corinthians: 4:6 – 9

We are afflicted, but not crushed

For God who said, "Let light shine out of darkness," has shone in our hearts to bring to light the knowledge of the glory of God on the face of Jesus Christ.

But we hold this treasure in earthen vessels, that the surpassing power may be of God and not from us. We are afflicted in every way, but not constrained; perplexed, but not driven to despair; persecuted, but not abandoned; struck down, but not destroyed.

417   Or:

Isaiah 63:7 – 9 — He has favored us according to his mercy.

Romans 8:18 – 25 — I consider the sufferings of the present to be as nothing compared with the glory to be revealed in us.

Matthew 15:21 – 28 — Woman, you have great faith.

418   As circumstances suggest, one of the following responsorial psalms may be sung or said, or some other suitable song.

R. *Our help is from the Lord who made heaven and earth.*

Psalm 121

I lift up my eyes toward the mountains;
whence shall help come to me?

My help is from the LORD
who made heaven and earth. **R.**

May he not suffer your foot to slip;
may he slumber not who guards you:
Indeed he neither slumbers nor sleeps,
the guardian of Israel. **R.**

The LORD is your guardian; the LORD is your shade;
he is beside you at your right hand.
The sun shall not harm you by day,
nor the moon by night. **R.**

The LORD will guard you from all evil;
he will guard your life.
the LORD will guard your coming and your going,
both now and forever. **R.**

Psalm 130:1–2, 3–4, 5–6, 7–8
R. *(v. 5) My soul trusts in the Lord.*

419   *As circumstances suggest, the minister may give those present a brief
explanation of the biblical text, so that they may understand through faith the
meaning of the celebration.*

INTERCESSIONS

420   *The intercessions are then said. The minister introduces them and an
assisting minister or one of those present announces the intentions. From the
following those best suited to the occasion may be used or adapted, or other
intentions that apply to the particular circumstances may be composed.*

The minister says:

Our God gives us life and constantly calls us to new life; let us pray to God with confidence.
R. *Lord, hear our prayer.*

Assisting minister:

For those addicted to alcohol/drugs, that God may be their strength and support, we pray. **R.**

Assisting minister:

For **N.**, bound by the chains of addiction/substance abuse, that we encourage and assist him/her in his/her struggle, we pray. **R.**

Assisting minister:

For **N.**, that he/she may trust in the mercy of God through whom all things are possible, we pray. **R.**

Assisting minister:

For the family and friends of **N.**, that with faith and patience they show him/her their love, we pray. **R.**

Assisting minister:

For the Church, that it may always be attentive to those in need, we pray. **R.**

421   *After the intercessions the minister, in the following or similar words, invites all present to sing or say the Lord's Prayer.*
Let us pray to our merciful God as Jesus taught us:
All:
Our Father . . .

PRAYER OF BLESSING

422   A minister who is a priest or deacon says the prayer of blessing with hands outstretched over the person; a lay minister says the prayer with hands joined.

A   *For addiction*

God of mercy,
we bless you in the name of your Son, Jesus Christ,
who ministered to all who came to him.
Give your strength to N., your servant,
bound by the chains of addiction.
Enfold him/her in your love
and restore him/her to the freedom of God's children.

Lord,
look with compassion on all those
who have lost their health and freedom.
Restore to them the assurance of your
        unfailing mercy,
and strengthen them in the work of recovery.

To those who care for them,
grant patient understanding and a love
        that perseveres.

We ask this through Christ our Lord.
R. Amen.

B   *For substance abuse*

God of mercy,
we bless you in the name of your Son, Jesus Christ,
who ministered to all who came to him.
Give your strength to **N.**, your servant,
enfold him/her in your love
and restore him/her to the freedom of God's children.

Lord,
look with compassion on all those
who have lost their health and freedom.
Restore to them the assurance of your
        unfailing mercy,
strengthen them in the work of recovery,
and help them to resist all temptation.

To those who care for them,
grant patient understanding and a love
        that perseveres.

We ask this through Christ our Lord.
R. Amen.

As circumstances suggest, the minister in silence may sprinkle the person with holy water.

CONCLUDING RITE

424   *A lay minister concludes the rite by signing himself or herself with the sign of the cross and saying:*

May our all-merciful God, Father, Son, and Holy Spirit, bless us and embrace us in love for ever.
R. Amen.

425   *It is preferable to end the celebration with a suitable song.*

B. SHORTER RITE

426   *All make the sign of the cross as the minister says:*

Our help is in the name of the Lord.

All reply:

Who made heaven and earth.

427   *One of those present or the minister reads a text of sacred Scripture, for example:*

Brothers and sisters, listen to the words of the second letter of Paul to the Corinthians: 4:6 – 9

We are afflicted, but not crushed

For God who said, "Let light shine out of darkness," has shone in our hearts to bring to light the knowledge of the glory of God on the face of Jesus Christ.

But we hold this treasure in earthen vessels, that the surpassing power may be of God and not from us. We are afflicted in every way, but not constrained; perplexed, but not driven to despair; persecuted, but not abandoned; struck down, but not destroyed.

428 Or:

Isaiah 63:7–9—He has favored us according to his mercy.

Matthew 15:21–28—Woman, you have great faith.

429   *A minister who is a priest or deacon says the prayer of blessing with hands outstretched over the person; a lay minister says the prayer with hands joined.*

A   *For addiction*

God of mercy,
we bless you in the name of your Son, Jesus Christ,
who ministered to all who came to him.
Give your strength to N., your servant,
bound by the chains of addiction.
Enfold him/her in your love
and restore him/her to the freedom of God's children.

Lord,
look with compassion on all those
who have lost their health and freedom.
Restore to them the assurance of your
        unfailing mercy,
and strengthen them in the work of your recovery.

To those who care for them,
grant patient understanding and a love
        that perseveres.

We ask this through Christ our Lord.
R. Amen.

B *For substance abuse.*

God of mercy,
we bless you in the name of your Son, Jesus Christ,
who ministered to all who came to him.
Give your strength to *N.*, your servant,
enfold him/her in your love
and restore him/her to the freedom of God's children.

Lord,
look with compassion on all those
who have lost their health and freedom.
Restore to them the assurance of your
        unfailing mercy,
strengthen them in the work of recovery,
and help them to resist all temptation.

To those who care for them,
grant patient understanding and a love
        that perseveres.

We ask this through Christ our Lord.
R. Amen.

Order for the Blessing of a Victim of Crime or Oppression

INTRODUCTION

430   The personal experience of a crime, political oppression, or social oppression can be traumatic and not easily forgotten. A victim often needs the assistance of others, and no less that of God, in dealing with this experience.

431   This blessing is intended to assist the victim and help him or her come to a state of tranquility and peace.

432   These orders may be used by a priest or a deacon, and also by a layperson, who follows the rites and prayers designated for a lay minister.

A. ORDER OF BLESSING

INTRODUCTORY RITES

433   *When the community has gathered, a suitable song may be sung. After the singing, the minister says:*

In the name of the Father, and of the Son, and of the Holy Spirit.

All make the sign of the cross and reply:

Amen.

435   *A lay minister greets those present in the following words:*

May the Lord grant us peace, now and for ever.

R. Amen.

436   *In the following or similar words, the minister prepares those present for the blessing.*

Throughout history God has manifested his love and care for those who have suffered from violence, hatred, and oppression. We commend N. to the healing mercy of God who binds up all our wounds and enfolds us in his gentle care.

READING OF THE WORD OF GOD

437   *A reader, another person present, or the minister reads a text of sacred Scripture.*

Brothers and sisters, listen to the words of the holy gospel according to Matthew: 10:28–33

Do not fear.

Jesus said to his disciples: "Do not be afraid of those who kill the body but cannot kill the soul; rather, be afraid of the one who can destroy both soul and body in Gehenna. Are not two sparrows sold for a small coin? Yet not one of them falls to the ground without your Father's knowledge. Even all the hairs of your head are counted. So do not be afraid; you are worth more than many sparrows. Everyone who acknowledges me before others I will acknowledge before my heavenly Father. But whoever denies me before others, I will deny before my heavenly Father."

438   *Or:*

Isaiah 59:6b–8, 15–18—*The Lord is appalled by evil and injustice.*

Job 3:1–26—*Lamentation of Job.*

Lamentations 3:1–24—*I am one who knows affliction.*

Lamentations 3:49–59—*When I called, you came to my aid.*

Micah 4:1–4—*Every person shall sit undisturbed.*

Matthew 5:1–10—*The beatitudes.*

Matthew 5:43–48—*Love your enemies, pray for those who persecute you.*

Luke 10:25–37—*The good Samaritan.*

439   *As circumstances suggest, one of the following responsorial psalms may be sung, or some other suitable song.*

R. The Lord is my strength and my salvation.

Psalm 140

Deliver me, O LORD, from evil men;
preserve me from violent men,
From those who devise evil in their hearts,
and stir up wars ever day. **R.**

Save me, O LORD, from the hands of the wicked;
preserve me from violent men
Who plan to trip up my feet —
the proud who have hidden a trap for me;
They have spread cords for a net;
by the wayside they have laid snares for me. **R.**

Grant not, O LORD, the desires of the wicked;
further not their plans.
Those who surround me lift up their heads;
may the mischief which they threaten
      overwhelm them. **R.**

I know that the LORD renders
justice to the afflicted, judgment to the poor.
Surely the just shall give thanks to your name;
the upright shall dwell in your presence. **R.**

Psalm 12:2–3, 4b–5, 6–7
R. *(v. 6) You, O Lord, are my refuge.*

Psalm 31:2–3a, 4–5, 15–16, 24–25
R. *(v. 6) Into your hands I commend my spirit.*

440   *As circumstances suggest, the minister may give those present a brief explanation of the biblical text, so that they may understand through faith the meaning of the celebration.*

INTERCESSIONS

441   *The intercessions are then said. The minister introduces them and an assisting minister or one of those present announces the intentions. From the*

following those best suited to the occasion may be used or adapted, or other intentions that apply to the particular circumstances may be composed.

The minister says:

Let us pray to the Lord God, the defender of the weak and powerless, who delivered our ancestors from harm.

R. *Deliver us from evil, O Lord.*

Assisting minister:

For **N.**, that he/she may be freed from pain and fear, we pray to the Lord. **R.**

Assisting minister:

For all who are victims of crime/oppression, we pray to the Lord. **R.**

Assisting minister:

For an end to all acts of violence and hatred, we pray to the Lord. **R.**

Assisting minister:

For those who harm others, that they may change their lives and turn to God, we pray to the Lord. R.

442   *After the intercessions the minister, in the following or similar words, invites all present to sing or say the Lord's Prayer.*

The Lord heals our wounds and strengthens us in our weakness; let us pray as Christ has taught us:

All:

Our Father . . .

Prayer of Blessing

443 *A minister who is a priest or deacon says the prayer of blessing with hands outstretched over the person to be blessed; a lay minister says the prayer with hands joined.*

Lord God,
your own Son was delivered into the hands of
    the wicked,
yet he prayed for his persecutors
and overcame hatred with the blood of the cross.
Relieve the suffering of N.;
grant him/her peace of mind
and a renewed faith in your protection and care.

Protect us all from the violence of others,
keep us safe from the weapons of hate,
and restore to us tranquility and peace.

We ask this through Christ our Lord.
R. Amen.

As circumstances suggest, the minister in silence may sprinkle the person with holy water.

Concluding Rite

445 *A lay minister concludes the rite by signing himself or herself with the sing of the cross and saying:*
May God bless us with his mercy,
strengthen us with his love,
and enable us to walk in charity and peace.
R. Amen.

446 *It is preferable to end the celebration with a suitable song.*

SHORTER RITE

447 *All make the sign of the cross as the minister says:*

Our help is in the name of the Lord.

All reply:

Who made heaven and earth.

448 *One of those present or the minister reads a text of sacred Scripture, for example:*

Brothers and sisters, listen to the words of the holy gospel according to Matthew: 10:28–33

Do not fear.

Jesus said to his disciples: "Do not be afraid of those who kill the body but cannot kill the soul; rather, be afraid of the one who can destroy both soul and body in Gehenna. Are not two sparrows sold for a small coin? Yet not one of them falls to the ground without your Father's knowledge. Even all the hairs of your head are counted. So do not be afraid; you are worth more than many sparrows. Everyone who acknowledges me before others I will acknowledge before my heavenly Father. But whoever denies me before others, I will deny before my heavenly Father."

449 *Or:*

Isaiah 59:6b–8, 15–18 — The Lord is appalled by evil and injustice.

Job 3:1–26 — Lamentation of Job.

Lamentations 3:1–24 — I am a man who knows affliction.

Lamentations 3:49–59 — When I called, you came to my aid.

Matthew 5:1–10 — The beatitudes.

Luke 10:25–37 — The good Samaritan.

450 *A minister who is a priest or deacon says the prayer of blessing with hands outstretched over the person; a lay minister says the prayer with hands joined.*

Lord God,
your own Son was delivered into the hands of
     the wicked
yet he prayed for his persecutors
and overcame hatred with the blood of the cross.
Relive the suffering of N.;
grant him/her peace of mind
and a renewed faith in your protection and care.

Protect us all from the violence of others,
keep us safe from the weapons of hate,
and restore to us tranquility and peace.

We ask this through Christ our Lord.
R. Amen.

Order for the Blessing of Parents after a Miscarriage

INTRODUCTION

279   In times of death and grief the Christian turns to the Lord for consolation and strength. This is especially true when a child dies before birth. This blessing is provided to assist the parents in their grief and console them with the blessing of God.

280   The minister should be attentive to the needs of the parents and other family members and to this end the introduction to the *Order of Christian Funerals,* Part II: Funeral Rites for Children will be helpful.

281   These orders may be used by a priest or deacon, and also by a layperson who follows the rites and prayers designated for a lay minister.

A. ORDER OF BLESSING

INTRODUCTORY RITES

282   When the community has gathered, a suitable song may be sung. The minister says:

In the name of the Father, and of the Son, and of the Holy Spirit.

All make the sign of the cross and reply:

Amen.

284   A lay minister greets those present in the following words:

Let us praise the Father of mercies, the God of all consolation. Blessed be God for ever.

R. Blessed be God for ever.

285   In the following or similar words, the minister prepares those present for the blessing.

For those who trust in God,
in the pain of sorrow there is consolation,
in the face of despair there is hope,
in the midst of death there is life.
N. and N., as we mourn the death of your child we place ourselves in the hands of God and ask for strength, for healing, and for love.

READING OF THE WORD OF GOD

286   A reader, another person present, or the minister reads a text of sacred Scripture.

Brothers and sisters, listen to the words of the book of Lamentations: 3:17–26

Hope in the Lord.

My soul is deprived of peace,
I have forgotten what happiness is;
I tell myself my future is lost,
all that I hoped for from the Lord.
The thought of my homeless poverty
is wormwood and gall;
Remembering it over and over
leaves my soul downcast within me.
But I will call this to mind,
as my reason to have hope:
The favors of the LORD are not exhausted,
his mercies are not spent;
They are renewed each morning,
so great is his faithfulness.
My portion is the LORD, says my soul;
therefore will I hope in him.
Good is the LORD to one who waits for him,
to the soul that seeks him;
It is good to hope in silence
for the saving help of the LORD.

287   Or:

*Isaiah 49:8–13 — In a time of favor I answer you, on the day of salvation
I help you.*

Romans 8:18–27 — In hope we were saved.

Romans 8:26–31 — If God is for us, who can be against us?

Colossians 1:9–12 — We have been praying for you unceasingly.

Hebrews 5:7–10—Christ intercedes for us.

Luke 22:39–46—Agony in the garden.

288   *As circumstances suggest, one of the following responsorial psalms may be sung, or some other suitable song.*

R. *To you, O Lord, I lift up my soul.*

Psalm 25

Your ways, O LORD, make known to me;
teach me your paths,
Guide me in your truth and teach me,
for you are God my savior,
and for you I wait all the day. **R.**

Remember that your compassion, O LORD,
and your kindness are from of old.
The sins of my youth and my frailties remember not;
in your kindness remember me
because of your goodness, O LORD. **R.**

Look toward me, and have pity on me,
for I am alone and afflicted.
Relieve the troubles of my heart,
and bring me out of my distress. **R.**

Preserve my life, and rescue me;
let me not be put to shame, for I take refuge in you.
Let integrity and uprightness preserve me,
because I wait for you, O LORD. **R.**

Psalm 143:1, 5–6, 8, 30

R. *(v. 1) O Lord, hear my prayer.*

289   As circumstances suggest, the minister may give those present a brief explanation of the biblical text, so that they may understand through faith the meaning of the celebration.

INTERCESSIONS

290   The intercessions are then said. The minister introduces them and an assisting minister or one of those present announces the intentions. From the following those best suited to the occasion may be used or adapted, or other intentions that apply to the particular circumstances may be composed.

The minister says:

Let us pray to God who throughout the ages has heard the cries of parents.
R. *Lord, hear our prayer.*

Assisting minister:

For N. and N., who know the pain of grief, that they may be comforted, we pray. R.

Assisting minister:

For this family, that it may find new hope in the midst of suffering, we pray. R.

Assisting minister:

For these parents, that they may learn from the example of Mary, who grieved by the cross of her Son, we pray. R.

Assisting minister:

For all who have suffered the loss of a child, that Christ may be their support, we pray. R.

291   *After the intercessions the minister, in the following or similar words, invites all present to sing or say the Lord's Prayer.*

Let us pray to the God of consolation and hope, as Christ has taught us:

All:

Our Father . . .

PRAYER OF BLESSING

292   *A minister who is a priest or deacon says the prayer of blessing with hands outstretched over the parents; a lay minister says the prayer with hands joined.*

Compassionate God,
soothe the hearts of *N.* and *N.*,
and grant that through the prayers of Mary,
who grieved by the cross of her Son,
you may enlighten their faith,
give hope to their hearts,
and peace to their lives.

Lord,
grant mercy to all the members of this family
and comfort them with the hope
that one day we will all live with you,
with your Son Jesus Christ, and the Holy Spirit,
for ever and ever.
R. Amen.

293   *Or:*

Lord,
God of all creation
we bless and thank you for your tender care.

Receive this life you created in love
and comfort your faithful people in their time of loss
with the assurance of your unfailing mercy.

We ask this through Christ our Lord.
R. Amen.

As circumstances suggest, the minister in silence may sprinkle the parents with holy water.

CONCLUDING RITE

295   A lay minister concludes the rite by signing himself or herself with the sing of the cross and saying:

May God give us peace in our sorrow,
consolation in our grief,
and strength to accept his will in all things.
R. Amen.

296   It is preferable to end the celebration with a suitable song.

SHORTER RITE

297   All make the sign of the cross as the minister says:

Our help is in the name of the Lord.

All reply:

Who made heaven and earth.

**Brothers and sisters, listen to the words of the book
of Lamentations:**   3:17-26

Hope in the Lord.

My soul is deprived of peace,
I have forgotten what happiness is;
I tell myself my future is lost,
all that I hoped for from the LORD.
The thought of my homeless poverty
is wormwood and gall;
Remembering it over and over
leaves my soul downcast within me.
But I will call this to mind,
as my reason to have hope:
The favors of the LORD are not exhausted,
his mercies are not spent;
They are renewed each morning,
so great is his faithfulness.
My portion is the LORD, says my soul;
therefore will I hope in him.
Good is the LORD to one who waits for him,
to the soul that seeks him;
It is good to hope in silence
for the saving help of the LORD.

299   Or:

Romans 8:26-31 — If God is for us, who can be against us?

Colossians 1:9-12 — We have been praying for you unceasingly.

300   *A minister who is a priest or deacon says the prayer of blessing with hands outstretched over the parents; a lay minister says the prayer with hands joined.*

Compassionate God,
soothe the hearts of **N.** and **N.**,
and grant that through the prayers of Mary,
who grieved by the cross of her Son,
you may enlighten their faith,
give hope to their hearts,
and peace to their lives.

Lord,
grant mercy to all the members of this family
and comfort them with the hope
that one day we will all live with you,
with your Son Jesus Christ, and the Holy Spirit,
for ever and ever.
R. Amen.

301   *Or:*
Lord,
God of all creation,
we bless and thank you for your tender care.
Receive this life you created in love
and comfort your faithful people in their time of loss
with the assurance of your unfailing mercy.

We ask this through Christ our Lord.
R. Amen.

Pastoral Care of the Sick

INTRODUCTION

Lord, your friend is sick.

42   The rites in Part I of *Pastoral Care of the Sick: Rites of Anointing and Viaticum* are used by the Church to comfort the sick in time of anxiety, to encourage them to fight against illness, and perhaps to restore them to health. These rites are distinct from those in the second part of this book, which are provided to comfort and strengthen a Christian in the passage from this life.

43   The concern that Christ showed for the bodily and spiritual welfare of those who are ill is continued by the Church in its ministry to the sick. This ministry is the common responsibility of all Christians, who should visit the sick, remember them in prayer, and celebrate the sacraments with them. The family and friends of the sick, doctors and others who care for them, and priests with pastoral responsibilities have a particular share in this ministry of comfort. Through words of encouragement and faith they can help the sick to unite themselves with the sufferings of Christ for the good of God's people.

Remembrance of the sick is especially appropriate at common worship on the Lord's Day, during the general intercessions at Mass and in the intercessions at Morning Prayer and Evening Prayer. Family members and those who are dedicated to the care of the sick should be remembered on these occasions as well.

44   Priests have the special task of preparing the sick to celebrate the sacrament of penance (individually or in a communal celebration), to receive the eucharist frequently if their condition permits, and to celebrate the sacrament of anointing at the appropriate time. During this preparation it will be especially helpful if the sick person, the priest, and the family become accustomed to praying together. The priest should provide leadership to those who assist him in the care of the sick, especially deacons and other ministers of the eucharist.

The words "priest," "deacon," and "minister" are used advisedly. Only in those rites which must be celebrated by a priest is the word "priest" used in the rubrics (that is, the sacrament of penance, the sacrament of the anointing of the sick, the celebration of viaticum within Mass). Whenever it is clear that, in the absence of a priest, a deacon may preside at a particular rite, the words "priest or deacon" are used in the rubrics. Whenever another minister is permitted to celebrate a rite in the absence of a priest or deacon, the word "minister" is used in the rubrics, even though in many cases the rite will be celebrated by a priest or deacon.

45   The pastoral care of the sick should be suited to the nature and length of the illness. An illness of short duration in which the full recovery of health is a possibility requires a more intensive ministry, whereas illness of a longer duration which may be a prelude to death requires a more extensive ministry. An awareness of the attitudes and emotional states which these different situations engender in the sick is indispensable to the development of an appropriate ministry.

VISITS TO THE SICK
46   Those who visit the sick should help them to pray, sharing with them the word of God proclaimed in the assembly

from which their sickness has separated them. As the occasion permits, prayer drawn from the psalms or from other prayers or litanies may be added to the word of God. Care should be taken to prepare for a future visit during which the sick will receive the eucharist.

VISITS TO A SICK CHILD

47   What has already been said about visiting the sick and praying with them (see no. 46) applies also in visits to a sick child. Every effort should be made to know the child and to accommodate the care in keeping with the age and comprehension of the child. In these circumstances the minister should also be particularly concerned to help the child's family.

48   If it is appropriate, the priest may discuss with the parents the possibility of preparing and celebrating with the child the sacraments of initiation (baptism, confirmation, eucharist). The priest may baptize and confirm the child (see *Rite of Confirmation*, no. 7b). To complete the process of initiation, the child should also receive first communion. (If the child is a proper subject for confirmation, then he or she may receive first communion in accordance with the practice of the Church.) There is no reason to delay this, especially if the illness is likely to be a long one.

49   Throughout the illness the minister should ensure that the child receives communion frequently, making whatever adaptations seem necessary in the rite for communion of the sick (Chapter III).

50   The child is to be anointed if he or she has sufficient use of reason to be strengthened by the sacrament of anointing. The rites provided (Chapter IV) are to be used and adapted.

COMMUNION OF THE SICK

51 Because the sick are prevented from celebrating the eucharist with the rest of the community, the most important visits are those during which they receive holy communion. In receiving the body and blood of Christ, the sick are united sacramentally to the Lord and are reunited with the eucharistic community from which illness has separated them.

ANOINTING OF THE SICK

52 The priest should be especially concerned for those whose health has been seriously impaired by illness or old age. He will offer them a new sign of hope: the laying on of hands and the anointing of the sick accompanied by the prayer of faith (James 5:14). Those who receive this sacrament in the faith of the Church will find it a true sign of comfort and support in time of trial. It will work to overcome the sickness, if this is God's will.

53 Some types of mental sickness are now classified as serious. Those who are judged to have a serious mental illness and who would be strengthened by the sacrament may be anointed (see no. 5). The anointing may be repeated in accordance with the conditions for other kinds of serious illness (see no. 9).

Visits to the Sick

INTRODUCTION

I was sick, and you visited me

54   The prayers contained in this chapter follow the common pattern of reading, response, prayer, and blessing. This pattern is provided as an example of what can be done and may be adapted as necessary. The minister may wish to invite those present to prepare for the reading from Scripture, perhaps by a brief introduction or through a moment of silence. The laying on of hands may be added by the priest, if appropriate, after the blessing is given.

55   The sick should be encouraged to pray when they are alone or with their families, friends, or those who care for them. Their prayer should be drawn primarily from Scripture. The sick person and others may help to plan the celebration, for example, by choosing the prayers and readings. Those making these choices should keep in mind the condition of the sick person.

The passages found in this chapter and those included in Part III speak of the mystery of human suffering in the words, works, and life of Christ. Occasionally, for example, on the Lord's Day, the sick may feel more involved in the worship of the community from which they are separated if the readings used are those assigned for that day in the lectionary. Prayers may also be drawn from the psalms or from other prayers or litanies. The sick should be helped in making this form of prayer, and the minister should always be ready to pray with them.

56   The minister should encourage the sick person to offer his or her sufferings in union with Christ and to join in prayer for the Church and the world. Some examples of particular intentions which may be suggested to the sick person are: for peace in the world; for a deepening of the life of the Spirit in the local Church; for the pope and the bishops; for people suffering in a particular disaster.

VISITS TO THE SICK

READING

57   *The word of God is proclaimed by one of those present or by the minister.*
An appropriate reading from Part III or one of the following readings may
be used:

A   Acts of the Apostles 3:1–10

In the name of Jesus and the power of his Church, there is salvation —
even liberation from sickness.

B   Matthew 8:14–17

Jesus fulfills the prophetic figure of the servant of God taking upon himself and
relieving the sufferings of God's people.

RESPONSE

58   *A brief period of silence may be observed after the reading of the word*
of God. An appropriate psalm from Part III or one of the following psalms may
be used:

A   *Psalm 102*

R. *O Lord, hear my prayer and*
        let my cry come to you.

O LORD, hear my prayer,
        and let my cry come to you.

Hide not your face from me
    in the day of my distress.
Incline your ear to me;
    in the day when I call, answer me speedily.

*R. O Lord, hear my prayer and
    let my cry come to you.*

He has broken down my strength in the way;
    he has cut short my days.
        I say: O my God,
Take me not hence in the midst of my days;
    through all generations your years endure.

*R. O Lord, hear my prayer and
    let my cry come to you.*

Of old you established the earth,
    and the heavens are the work of your hands.
They shall perish, but you remain
    though all of them grow old like a garment.
Like clothing you change them, and they are changed,
    but you are the same,
and your years have no end.

*R. O Lord, hear my prayer and
    let my cry come to you.*

Let this be written for the generation to come,
    and let his future creatures praise the LORD:

"The LORD looked down from his holy height,
    from heaven he beheld the earth,
To hear the groaning of the prisoners,
    to release those doomed to die."

R. *O Lord, hear my prayer and*
    let my cry come to you.

B   *Psalm 27*

R. *The Lord is my light and my salvation.*

The LORD is my light and my salvation;
    whom should I fear?
The LORD is my life's refuge;
    of whom should I be afraid?

R. *The Lord is my light and my salvation.*

One thing I ask of the LORD;
    this I seek:
To dwell in the house of the LORD
    all the days of my life
That I may gaze on the loveliness of the LORD
    and contemplate his temple.

R. *The Lord is my light and my salvation.*

For he will hide me in his abode
    in the day of trouble,

He will conceal me in the shelter of his tent,
     he will set me high upon a rock.

R. *The Lord is my light and my salvation.*

The minister may then give a brief explanation of the reading, applying it to the needs of the sick person and those who are looking after him or her.

THE LORD'S PRAYER

59   The minister introduces the Lord's Prayer in these or similar words:

Now let us offer together the prayer our Lord Jesus Christ taught us:

All say:

Our Father . . .

CONCLUDING PRAYER

60   The minister says a concluding prayer. One of the following may be used:

A

Father,
your Son accepted our sufferings
to teach us the virtue of patience in human illness.
Hear the prayers we offer for our sick brother/sister.
May all who suffer pain, illness, or disease realize
that they have been chosen to be saints and know

that they are joined to Christ in his suffering for the salvation of the world.

We ask this through Christ our Lord.
R. *Amen.*

B
All-powerful and ever-living God,
the lasting health of all who believe in you,
hear us as we ask your loving help for the sick;
restore their health,
that they may again offer joyful thanks
      in your Church.

Grant this through Christ our Lord.
R. *Amen.*

C
All-powerful and ever-living God,
we find security in your forgiveness.
Give us serenity and peace of mind;
may we rejoice in your gifts of kindness
and use them always for your glory and our good.

We ask this in the name of Jesus the Lord.
R. *Amen.*

BLESSING

The minister may give a blessing. One of the following may be used:

A

All praise and glory is yours, Lord our God,
for you have called us to serve you in love.
Bless **N.**
so that he/she may bear this illness
in union with your Son's obedient suffering.
Restore him/her to health,
and lead him/her to glory.

We ask this through Christ our Lord.
R. Amen.

B

For an elderly person

All praise and glory are yours, Lord our God,
for you have called us to serve you in love.
Bless all who have grown old in your service
and give **N.** strength and courage
to continue to follow Jesus your Son.

We ask this through Christ our Lord.
R. Amen.

A minister who is not a priest or deacon invokes God's blessing and makes the sign of the cross on himself or herself, while saying:

May the Lord bless us,
protect us from all evil,
and bring us to everlasting life.
R. Amen.

The minister may then trace the sign of the cross on the sick person's forehead.

Visits To A Sick Child

INTRODUCTION

Let the children come to me; do not keep them back from me.

62   The following readings, prayers, and blessings will help the minister to pray with sick children and their families. They are provided as an example of what can be done and may be adapted as necessary. The minister may wish to invite those present to prepare for the reading from Scripture, perhaps by a brief introduction or through a moment of silence.

63   If the child does not already know the minister, the latter should seek to establish a friendly and easy relationship with the child. Therefore, the greeting which begins the visit should be an informal one.

64   The minister should help sick children to understand that the sick are very special in the eyes of God because they are suffering as Christ suffered and because they can offer their sufferings for the salvation of the world.

65   In praying with the sick child the minister chooses, together with the child and the family if possible, suitable elements of common prayer in the form of a brief liturgy of the word. This may consist of a reading from Scripture, simple one-line prayers taken from Scripture which can be repeated by the child, other familiar prayers such as the Lord's Prayer, the Hail Mary, litanies, or a simple form of the general intercessions. The laying on of hands may be added by the priest, if appropriate, after the child has been blessed.

READING

66   *One of the following readings may be used for a brief liturgy of the word. Other readings may be chosen, for example: Mark 5:21–23, 35–43, Jesus raises the daughter of Jairus and gives her back to her parents; Mark 9:14–27, Jesus cures a boy and gives him back to his father; Luke 7:11–15, Jesus raises a young man, the only son of his mother, and gives him back to her; John 4:46–53, Jesus gives his second sign by healing an official's son. In addition, other stories concerning the Lord's healing ministry may be found suitable, especially if told with the simplicity and clarity of one of the children's versions of Scripture.*

A MARK 9:33–37
Jesus proposes the child as the ideal of those who would enter the kingdom.

B MARK 10:13–16
Jesus welcomes the children and lays hands on them.

RESPONSE

67   *After the reading of the word of God, time may be set apart for silent reflection if the child is capable of this form of prayer. The minister should also explain the meaning of the reading to those present, adapting it to their circumstances.*

The minister may then help the child and the family to respond to the word of God. The following short responsory may be used:

Jesus, come to me.

—Jesus, come to me.

Jesus, put your hand on me.

—Jesus, put your hand on me.

Jesus, bless me.

—*Jesus, bless me.*

THE LORD'S PRAYER

68   *The minister introduces the Lord's Prayer in these or similar words:*

Let us pray to the Father using those words which Jesus himself used:

All say:

Our Father . . .

CONCLUDING PRAYER

69   *The minister says a concluding prayer. One of the following may be used.*

A

God of love,
ever caring,
ever strong,
stand by us in our time of need.

Watch over your child **N.** who is sick,
look after him/her in every danger,
and grant him/her your healing and peace.

We ask this in the name of Jesus the Lord.
R. Amen.

B

Father,
in your love
you gave us Jesus
to help us rise triumphant over grief and pain.

Look on your child N. who is sick
and see in his/her sufferings those of your Son.

Grant N. a share in the strength you granted your Son
that he/she too may be a sign
of your goodness, kindness, and loving care.

We ask this in the name of Jesus the Lord.
R. Amen.

BLESSING

70   *The minister makes a sign of the cross on the child's forehead, saying one of the following:*

A

N., when you were baptized,
you were marked with the cross of Jesus.
I (we) make this cross ✚ on your forehead
and ask the Lord to bless you,
and restore you to health.
R. Amen.

B

All praise and glory is yours, heavenly God,
for you have called us to serve you in love.
Have mercy on us and listen to our prayer
as we ask you to help **N.**

Bless ✚ your beloved child,
and restore him/her to health
in the name of Jesus the Lord.

R. Amen.

Each one present may in turn trace the sign of the cross on the child's forehead, in silence.

A minister who is not a priest or deacon concludes as described in no. 61.

Communion of the Sick

INTRODUCTION

Whoever eats this bread will live for ever.

71   This chapter contains two rites: one for use when communion can be celebrated in the context of a liturgy of the word; the other, a brief communion rite for use in more restrictive circumstances, such as in hospitals.

72   Priests with pastoral responsibilities should see to it that the sick or aged, even though not seriously ill or in danger of death, are given every opportunity to receive the eucharist frequently, even daily, especially during the Easter season. They may receive communion at any hour. Those who care for the sick may receive communion with them, in accord with the usual norms. To provide frequent communion for the sick, it may be necessary to ensure that the community has a sufficient number of ministers of communion. The communion minister should wear attire appropriate to this ministry.

The sick person and others may help to plan the celebration, for example, by choosing the prayers and readings. Those making these choices should keep in mind the condition of the sick person. The readings and the homily should help those present to reach a deeper understanding of the mystery of human suffering in relation to the paschal mystery of Christ.

73   The faithful who are ill are deprived of their rightful and accustomed place in the eucharistic community. In bringing communion to them the minister of communion represents Christ and manifests faith and charity on behalf of the whole community toward those who cannot be present at the eucharist. For the sick the reception of communion is not only

a privilege but also a sign of support and concern shown by the Christian community for its members who are ill.

The links between the community's eucharistic celebration, especially on the Lord's Day, and the communion of the sick are intimate and manifold. Besides remembering the sick in the general intercessions at Mass, those present should be reminded occasionally of the significance of communion in the lives of those who are ill: union with Christ in his struggle with evil, his prayer for the world, and his love for the Father, and union with the community from which they are separated.

The obligation to visit and comfort those who cannot take part in the eucharistic assembly may be clearly demonstrated by taking communion to them from the community's eucharistic celebration. This symbol of unity between the community and its sick members has the deepest significance on the Lord's Day, the special day of the eucharistic assembly.

74   When the eucharist is brought to the sick, it should be carried in a pyx or small closed container. Those who are with the sick should be asked to prepare a table covered with a linen cloth upon which the blessed sacrament will be placed. Lighted candles are prepared and, where it is customary, a vessel of holy water. Care should be taken to make the occasion special and joyful.

Sick people who are unable to receive communion under the form of bread may receive it under the form of wine alone. If the wine is consecrated at a Mass not celebrated in the presence of the sick person, the blood of the Lord is kept in a properly covered vessel and is placed in the tabernacle after communion. The precious blood should be carried to the sick in a vessel which is closed in such a way as to eliminate all danger of spilling. If some of the precious blood remains, it should be consumed by the minister, who should also see to it that the vessel is properly purified.

75   If the sick wish to celebrate the sacrament of penance, it is preferable that the priest make himself available for this during a previous visit.

76   If it is necessary to celebrate the sacrament of penance during the rite of communion, it takes the place of the penitential rite.

COMMUNION IN ORDINARY CIRCUMSTANCES

77   If possible, provision should be made to celebrate Mass in the homes of the sick, with their families and friends gathered around them. The Ordinary determines the conditions and requirements for such celebrations.

COMMUNION IN A HOSPITAL OR INSTITUTION

78   There will be situations, particularly in large institutions with many communicants, when the minister should consider alternative means so that the rite of communion of the sick is not diminished to the absolute minimum. In such cases the following alternatives should be considered: (a) where possible, the residents or patients may be gathered in groups in one or more areas; (b) additional ministers of communion may assist.

When it is not possible to celebrate the full rite, the rite for communion in a hospital or institution may be used. If it is convenient, however, the minister may add elements from the rite for ordinary circumstances, for example, a Scripture reading.

79   The rite begins with the recitation of the eucharistic antiphon in the church, the hospital chapel, or the first room visited. Then the minister gives communion to the sick in their individual rooms.

80   The concluding prayer may be said in the church, the hospital chapel, or the last room visited. No blessing is given.

COMMUNION IN ORDINARY CIRCUMSTANCES

INTRODUCTORY RITES

Greeting

81   The minister greets the sick person and the others present. One of the following may be used:

A

The peace of the Lord be with you always.
R. And also with you.

B

Peace be with you (this house) and with all who live here.
R. And also with you.

C

The grace of our Lord Jesus Christ and the love of God and the fellowship of the Holy Spirit be with you all.
R. And also with you.

D

The grace and peace of God our Father and the Lord
Jesus Christ be with you.
R. *And also with you.*

*The minister then places the blessed sacrament on the table, and all join in
adoration.*

PENITENTIAL RITE

83   *The minister invites the sick person and all present to join in the
penitential rite, using these or similar words:*

A

My brothers and sisters, to prepare ourselves for this
celebration, let us call to mind our sins.

B

My brothers and sisters, let us turn with confidence
to the Lord and ask his forgiveness for all our sins.

*After a brief period of silence, the penitential rite continues, using one of the
following:*

A

Lord Jesus, you healed the sick:
Lord, have mercy.
R. *Lord, have mercy.*

Lord Jesus, you forgave sinners:
Christ, have mercy.
R. *Christ, have mercy.*

Lord Jesus, you give us yourself to heal us
   and bring us strength:
Lord, have mercy.
R. *Lord, have mercy.*

B

All say:

I confess to almighty God,
and to you, my brothers and sisters,
that I have sinned through my own fault

They strike their breast.
in my thoughts and in my words,
in what I have done,
and in what I have failed to do;
and I ask blessed Mary, ever virgin,
all the angels and saints,
and you, my brothers and sisters,
to pray for me to the Lord our God.

The minister concludes the penitential rite with the following:
May almighty God have mercy on us,
forgive us our sins,
and bring us to everlasting life.
R. *Amen.*

LITURGY OF THE WORD
Reading

*84   The word of God is proclaimed by one of those present or by the minister.
An appropriate reading from Part III or one of the following readings may
be used:*

A John 6:51
B John 6:54–58
C John 14:6
D John 15:5
E John 4:16

Response

*85   A brief period of silence may be observed after the reading of the word
of God.*

*The minister may then give a brief explanation of the reading, applying it to the
needs of the sick person and those who are looking after him or her.*

GENERAL INTERCESSIONS

*86   The general intercessions may be said. With a brief introduction the
minister invites all those present to pray. After the intentions the minister says
the concluding prayer. It is desirable that the intentions be announced by
someone other than the minister.*

LITURGY OF HOLY COMMUNION
The Lord's Prayer

87   The minister introduces the Lord's Prayer in these or similar words:

A

Now let us pray as Christ the Lord has taught us:

B

And now let us pray with confidence as Christ our
Lord commanded:

All say:

Our Father . . .

Communion

88   *The minister shows the eucharistic bread to those present, saying:*

A

This is the bread of life.
Taste and see that the Lord is good.

B

This is the Lamb of God
who takes away the sins of the world.
Happy are those who are called to his supper.

The sick person and all who are to receive communion say:

Lord, I am not worthy to receive you,
but only say the word and I shall be healed.

The minister goes to the sick person and, showing the blessed sacrament, says:

The body of Christ.

The sick person answers: "Amen," and receives communion.

Then the minister says:

The blood of Christ.

The sick person answers: "Amen," and receives communion.
Others present who wish to receive communion then do so in the usual way.

After the conclusion of the rite, the minister cleanses the vessel as usual.

Silent Prayer

89   *Then a period of silence may be observed.*

Prayer after Communion

90   *The minister says a concluding prayer. One of the following may be used:*

Let us pray.

Pause for silent prayer, if this has not preceded.

A

God our Father,
you have called us to share the one bread
        and one cup
and so become one in Christ.

Help us to live in him
that we may bear fruit,
rejoicing that he has redeemed the world.

We ask this through Christ our Lord.
R. Amen.

B

All-powerful God,
we thank you for the nourishment you give us
through your holy gift.

Pour out your Spirit upon us
and in the strength of this food from heaven
keep us single-minded in your service.

We ask this in the name of Jesus the Lord.
R. Amen.

C
All-powerful and ever-living God,
may the body and blood of Christ your Son
be for our brother/sister **N.**
a lasting remedy for body and soul.

We ask this through Christ our Lord.
R. Amen.

CONCLUDING RITE
Blessing
91   *A minister who is not a priest or deacon invokes God's blessing and
makes the sign of the cross on himself or herself, while saying:*

A
May the Lord bless us,
protect us from all evil,
and bring us to everlasting life.
R. Amen.

B

May the almighty and merciful God bless and
protect us,
the Father, and the Son, ✝ and the Holy Spirit.
R. Amen.

COMMUNION IN A HOSPITAL OR INSTITUTION

INTRODUCTORY RITE

Antiphon

92   *The rite may begin in the church, the hospital chapel, or the first room, where the minister says one of the following antiphons:*

A

How holy this feast
in which Christ is our food:
his passion is recalled;
grace fills our hearts;
and we receive a pledge of the glory to come.

B

How gracious you are, Lord:
your gift of bread from heaven
reveals a Father's love and brings us perfect joy.
You fill the hungry with good things
and send the rich away empty.

C

I am the living bread
come down from heaven.
If you eat this bread
you will live for ever.

The bread I will give is my flesh
for the life of the world.

*If it is customary, the minister may be accompanied by a person carrying
a candle.*

Liturgy of Holy Communion
Greeting

93   *On entering each room, the minister may use one of the
following greetings:*

A

The peace of the Lord be with you always.
R. And also with you.

B

The grace of our Lord Jesus Christ and the love of
God and the fellowship of the Holy Spirit be with
you all.
R. And also with you.

*The minister then places the blessed sacrament on the table, and all join
in adoration.*

*If there is time and it seems desirable, the minister may proclaim
a scripture reading from those found in no. 84 or those appearing in Part III.*

The Lord's Prayer

94   *When circumstances permit (for example, when there are not many
rooms to visit), the minister is encouraged to lead the sick in the Lord's Prayer.
The minister introduces the Lord's Prayer in these or similar words:*

A

Jesus taught us to call God our Father, and so we
have the courage to say:

B

Now let us pray as Christ the Lord has taught us:

All say:

·Our Father . . .

Communion

95   *The minister shows the eucharistic bread to those present, saying:*

A

This is the Lamb of God
who takes away the sins of the world.
Happy are those who hunger and thirst,
for they shall be satisfied.

B

This it the bread of life,
Taste and see that the Lord is good.

The sick person and all who are to receive communion say:

Lord, I am not worthy to receive you,
but only say the word and I shall be healed.

The minister goes to the sick person and, showing the blessed sacrament, says:

The body of Christ.

The sick person answers: "Amen," and receives communion.

Then the minister says:

The blood of Christ.

The sick person answers: "Amen," and receives communion.

Others present who wish to receive communion then do so in the usual way.

CONCLUDING RITE
Concluding Prayer

96   *The concluding prayer may be said either in the last room visited, in the church, or chapel. One of the following may be used:*

Let us pray.

Pause for silent prayer.

A

God our Father,
you have called us to share the one bread
    and one cup
and so become one in Christ.

Help us to live in him
that we may bear fruit,
rejoicing that he has redeemed the world.

We ask this through Christ our Lord.
R. Amen.

B

All-powerful and ever-living God,
may the body and blood of Christ your Son
be for our brothers and sisters
a lasting remedy for body and soul.

We ask this through Christ our Lord.
R. Amen.

C

All-powerful God,
we thank you for the nourishment you give us
through your holy gift.

Pour out your Spirit upon us
and in the strength of this food from heaven
keep us single-minded in your service.

We ask this in the name of Jesus the Lord.
R. Amen.

The blessing is omitted and the minister cleanses the vessel as usual.

Pastoral Care of the Dying

INTRODUCTION

When we were baptized in Christ Jesus we were baptized into his death . . . so that as Christ was raised from the dead by the Father's glory, we too might live a new life.

161   The rites in Part II of *Pastoral Care of the Sick: Rites of Anointing and Viaticum* are used by the Church to comfort and strengthen a dying Christian in the passage from this life. The ministry to the dying places emphasis on trust in the Lord's promise of eternal life rather than on the struggle against illness which is characteristic of the pastoral care of the sick.

The first three chapters of Part II provide for those situations in which time is not a pressing concern and the rites can be celebrated fully and properly. These are to be clearly distinguished from the rites contained in Chapter Eight, "Rites for Exceptional Circumstances," which provide for the emergency situations sometimes encountered in the ministry to the dying.

162   Priests with pastoral responsibilities are to direct the efforts of the family and friends as well as other ministers of the local Church in the care of the dying. They should ensure that all are familiar with the rites provided here.

The words "priest," "deacon," and "minister" are used advisedly. Only in those rites which must be celebrated by a priest is the word "priest" used in the rubrics (that is, the sacrament of penance, the sacrament of the anointing of the sick, the celebration of viaticum within Mass). Whenever it is clear that, in the absence of a priest, a deacon may preside at a particular rite, the words "priest or deacon," are used in the rubrics. Whenever another minister is permitted to celebrate a rite in the absence of a priest or deacon, the word "minister" is used in the rubrics, even though in many cases the rite will be celebrated by a priest or deacon.

163   The Christian community has a continuing responsibility to pray for and with the person who is dying. Through its sacramental ministry to the dying the community helps Christians to embrace death in mysterious union with the crucified and risen Lord, who awaits them in the fullness of life.

CELEBRATION OF VIATICUM

164   A rite for viaticum within Mass and another for viaticum outside Mass are provided. If possible, viaticum should take place within the full eucharistic celebration, with the family, friends, and other members of the Christian community taking part. The rite for viaticum outside Mass is used when the full eucharistic celebration cannot take place. Again, if it is possible, others should take part.

COMMENDATION OF THE DYING

165   The second chapter of Part II contains a collection of prayers for the spiritual comfort of the Christian who is close to death. These prayers are traditionally called the commendation of the dying to God and are to be used according to the circumstances of each case.

PRAYERS FOR THE DEAD

166   A chapter has also been provided to assist a minister who has been called to attend a person who is already dead. A priest is not to administer the sacrament of anointing. Instead, he should pray for the dead person, using prayers such as

those which appear in this chapter. He may find it necessary to explain to the family of the person who is dead that sacraments are celebrated for the living, not for the dead, and that the dead are effectively helped by the prayers of the living.

RITES FOR EXCEPTIONAL CIRCUMSTANCES

167   Chapter Eight, "Rites for Exceptional Circumstances," contains rites which should be celebrated with a person who has suddenly been placed in proximate or immediate danger of death. They are for emergency circumstances and should be used only when such pressing conditions exist.

CARE OF A DYING CHILD

168   In its ministry to the dying the Church must also respond to the difficult circumstances of a dying child. Although no specific rites appear in Part II for the care of a dying child, these notes are provided to help bring into focus the various aspects of this ministry.

169   When parents learn that their child is dying, they are often bewildered and hurt. In their love for their son or daughter, they may be beset by temptations and doubts and find themselves asking: Why is God taking this child from us? How have we sinned or failed that God would punish us in this way? Why is this innocent child being hurt?

Under these trying circumstances, much of the Church's ministry will be directed to the parents and family. While pain and suffering in an innocent child are difficult for others to bear, the Church helps the parents and family to accept what God has allowed to happen. It should be understood by all beforehand that this process of acceptance will probably extend beyond the death of the child. The concern of the Christian community should continue as long as necessary.

Concern for the child must be equal to that for the family. Those who deal with dying children observe that their faith matures rapidly. Though young children often seem to accept death more easily than adults, they will often experience a surprisingly mature anguish because of the pain which they see in their families.

170   At such a time, it is important for members of the Christian community to come to the support of the child and the family by prayer, visits, and other forms of assistance. Those who have lost children of their own have a ministry of consolation and support to the family. Hospital personnel (doctors, nurses, aides) should also be prepared to exercise a special role with the child as caring adults. Priests and deacons bear particular responsibility for overseeing all these elements of the Church's pastoral ministry. The minister should invite members of the community to use their individual gifts in this work of communal care and concern.

171   By conversation and brief services of readings and prayers, the minister may help the parents and family to see that their child is being called ahead of them to enter the kingdom and joy of the Lord. The period when the child is dying can become a special time of renewal and prayer for the family and close friends. The minister should help them to see that the child's sufferings are united to those of Jesus for the salvation of the whole world.

172   If it is appropriate, the priest should discuss with the parents the possibility of preparing and celebrating with the child the sacraments of initiation (baptism, confirmation, eucharist). The priest may baptize and confirm the child (see·

Rite of Confirmation, no. 7b). To complete the process of initiation, the child should also receive first communion.

According to the circumstances, some of these rites may be celebrated by a deacon or layperson. So that the child and family may receive full benefit from them, these rites are normally celebrated over a period of time. In this case, the minister should use the usual rites, that is, the *Rite of Baptism for Children*, the *Rite of Confirmation*, and if suitable, the *Rite of Penance*. Similarly, if time allows, the usual rites for anointing and viaticum should be celebrated.

173   If sudden illness or an accident has placed an uninitiated child in proximate danger of death, the minister uses "Christian Initiation for the Dying," adapting it for use with a child.

174   For an initiated child or a child lacking only the sacrament of confirmation, who is in proximate danger of death, the "Continuous Rite of Penance, Anointing, and Viaticum" may be used and adapted to the understanding of the child. If death is imminent it should be remembered that viaticum rather than anointing is the sacrament for the dying.

CELEBRATION OF VIATICUM

INTRODUCTION

I am going to prepare a place for you; I shall come back and take you with me.

175   This chapter contains a rite for viaticum within Mass and a rite for viaticum outside Mass. The celebration of the eucharist as viaticum, food for the passage through death to eternal life, is the sacrament proper to the dying Christian. It is the completion and crown of the Christian life on this earth, signifying that the Christian follows the Lord to eternal glory and the banquet of the heavenly kingdom.

　　　The sacrament of the anointing of the sick should be celebrated at the beginning of a serious illness. Viaticum, celebrated when death is close, will then be better understood as the last sacrament of Christian life.

176   Priests and other ministers entrusted with the spiritual care of the sick should do everything they can to ensure that those in proximate danger of death receive the body and blood of Christ as viaticum. At the earliest opportunity, the necessary preparation should be given to the dying person, family, and others who may take part.

177   Whenever it is possible, the dying Christian should be able to receive viaticum within Mass. In this way he or she shares fully, during the final moments of this life, in the eucharistic sacrifice, which proclaims the Lord's own passing through death to life. However, circumstances, such as confinement to a hospital ward or the very emergency which makes death imminent, may frequently make the complete

eucharistic celebration impossible. In this case, the rite for viaticum outside Mass is appropriate. The minister should wear attire appropriate to this ministry.

178   Because the celebration of viaticum ordinarily takes place in the limited circumstances of the home, a hospital, or other institution, the simplifications of the rite for Masses in small gatherings may be appropriate. Depending on the condition of the dying person, every effort should be made to involve him or her, the family, friends, and other members of the local community in the planning and celebration. Appropriate readings, prayers, and songs will help to foster the full participation of all. Because of this concern for participation, the minister should ensure that viaticum is celebrated while the dying person is still able to take part and respond.

179   A distinctive feature of the celebration of viaticum, whether within or outside Mass, is the renewal of the baptismal profession of faith by the dying person. This occurs after the homily and replaces the usual form of the profession of faith. Through the baptismal profession at the end of earthly life, the one who is dying uses the language of his or her initial commitment, which is renewed each Easter and on other occasions in the Christian life. In the context of viaticum, it is a renewal and fulfillment of initiation into the Christian mysteries, baptism leading to the eucharist.

180   The rites for viaticum within and outside Mass may include the sign of peace. The minister and all who are present embrace the dying Christian. In this and in other parts of the celebration the sense of leave-taking need not be concealed or denied, but the joy of Christian hope, which is the comfort and strength of the one near death, should also be evident.

181   As an indication that the reception of the eucharist by the dying Christian is a pledge of resurrection and food for the passage through death, the special words proper to viaticum are added: "May the Lord Jesus Christ protect you and lead you to eternal life." The dying person and all who are present may receive communion under both kinds. The sign of communion is more complete when received in this manner because it expresses more fully and clearly the nature of the eucharist as a meal, one which prepares all who take part in it for the heavenly banquet (see the *General Instruction of the Roman Missal*, no. 240).

The minister should choose the manner of giving communion under both kinds which is suitable in the particular case. If the wine is consecrated at a Mass not celebrated in the presence of the sick person, the blood of the Lord is kept in a properly covered vessel and is placed in the tabernacle after communion. The precious blood should be carried to the sick person in a vessel which is closed in such a way as to eliminate all danger of spilling. If some of the precious blood remains after communion, it should be consumed by the minister, who should also see to it that the vessel is properly purified.

The sick who are unable to receive under the form of bread may receive under the form of wine alone. If the wine is consecrated at a Mass not celebrated in the presence of the sick person, the instructions given above are followed.

182   In addition to these elements of the rites which are to be given greater stress, special texts are provided for the general intercessions or litany and the final solemn blessing.

183   It often happens that a person who has received the eucharist as viaticum lingers in a grave condition or at the

point of death for a period of days or longer. In these circumstances he or she should be given the opportunity to receive the eucharist as viaticum on successive days, frequently if not daily. This may take place during or outside Mass as particular conditions permit. The rite may be simplified according to the condition of the one who is dying.

VIATICUM WITHIN MASS

184   When viaticum is received within Mass, the ritual Mass for Viaticum or the Mass of the Holy Eucharist may be celebrated. The priest wears white vestments. The readings may be taken from *The Lectionary for Mass* (second edition, nos. 796–800), unless the dying person and those involved with the priest in planning the liturgy choose other readings from Scripture.

A ritual Mass is not permitted during the Easter triduum, on the solemnities of Christmas, Epiphany, Ascension, Pentecost, Corpus Christi, or on a solemnity which is a holy day of obligation. On these occasions, the texts and readings are taken from the Mass of the day. Although the Mass for Viaticum or the Mass of the Holy Eucharist are also excluded on the Sundays of Advent, Lent, and the Easter season, on solemnities, Ash Wednesday, and the weekdays of Holy Week, one of the readings may be taken from the biblical texts indicated above. The special form of the final blessing may be used and, at the discretion of the priest, the apostolic pardon may be added.

185   If the dying person wishes to celebrate the sacrament of penance, it is preferable that the priest make himself available for this during a previous visit. If this is not possible, the sacrament of penance may be celebrated before Mass begins (see Appendix, p. 372).

VIATICUM OUTSIDE MASS

186   Although viaticum celebrated in the context of the full eucharistic celebration is always preferable, when it is not possible the rite for viaticum outside Mass is appropriate. This rite includes some of the elements of the Mass, especially a brief liturgy of the word. Depending on the circumstances and the condition of the dying person, this rite should also be a communal celebration. Every effort should be made to involve the dying person, family, friends, and members of the local community in the planning and celebration. The manner of celebration and the elements of the rite which are used should be accommodated to those present and the nearness of death.

187   If the dying person wishes to celebrate the sacrament of penance and this cannot take place during a previous visit, it should be celebrated before the rite of viaticum begins, especially if others are present. Alternatively, it may be celebrated during the rite of viaticum, replacing the penitential rite. At the discretion of the priest, the apostolic pardon may be added after the penitential rite or after the sacrament of penance.

188   An abbreviated liturgy of the word, ordinarily consisting of a single biblical reading, gives the minister an opportunity to explain the word of God in relation to viaticum. The sacrament should be described as the sacred food which strengthens the Christian for the passage through death to life in sure hope of the resurrection.

VIATICUM OUTSIDE MASS

INTRODUCTORY RITES

Greeting

197   *The minister greets the sick person and the others present. The following may be used:*

A

The peace of the Lord be with you always.

R. And also with you.

B

Peace be with you (this house) and with all who
live here.

R. And also with you.

C

The grace of our Lord Jesus Christ and the love of God
and the fellowship of the Holy Spirit be with you all.

R. And also with you.

D

The grace and peace of God our Father and the Lord
Jesus Christ be with you.

R. And also with you.

The minister then places the blessed sacrament on the table, and all join in adoration.

Instruction

199   Afterward the minister addresses those present, using the following instruction or one better suited to the sick person's condition:

My brothers and sisters, before our Lord Jesus Christ passed from this world to return to the Father, he left us the sacrament of his body and blood. When the hour comes for us to pass from this life and join him, he strengthens us with this food for our journey and comforts us by this pledge of our resurrection.

Penitential Rite

200   The minister invites the sick person and all present to join in the penitential rite, using these or similar words:

A

My brothers and sisters, to prepare ourselves for this celebration, let us call to mind our sins.

B

My brothers and sisters, let us turn with confidence to the Lord and ask his forgiveness for all our sins.

After a brief period of silence, the penitential rite continues using one of the following prayers.

A   *All say:*

I confess to almighty God,
and to you, my brothers and sisters,
that I have sinned through my own fault

They strike their breast.

in my thoughts and in my words,
in what I have done,
and in what I have failed to do;
and I ask blessed Mary, every virgin,
all the angels and saints,
and you, my brothers and sisters,
to pray for me to the Lord our God.

B

By your paschal mystery
      you have won for us salvation:
Lord, have mercy.
R. Lord, have mercy.

You renew among us now
      the wonders of your passion:
Christ, have mercy.
R. Christ, have mercy.

When we receive your body,
you share with us your paschal sacrifice:
Lord, have mercy.
R. Lord, have mercy.

The minister concludes the penitential rite with the following:

May almighty God have mercy us,
forgive us our sins,
and bring us to everlasting life.
R. Amen.

LITURGY OF THE WORD

Reading

*202   The word of God is proclaimed by one of those present or by the minister.
An appropriate reading from Part III or one of the following may be used:*

A John 6:54–55
B John 14:23
C John 15:4
D 1 Corinthians 11:26

Homily

*203   Depending on circumstances, the minister may then give a brief
explanation of the reading.*

Baptismal Profession of Faith

*204   It is desirable that the sick person renew his or her baptismal profession
of faith before receiving viaticum. The minister gives a brief introduction and
then asks the following questions:*

N., do you believe in God, the Father almighty,
creator of heaven and earth?
R. I do.

Do you believe in Jesus Christ, his only Son, our Lord,
who was born of the Virgin Mary,

was crucified, died, and was buried,
rose from the dead,
and is now seated at the right hand of the Father?
R. I do.

Do you believe in the Holy Spirit,
the holy catholic Church, the communion of saints,
the forgiveness of sins, the resurrection of the body,
and life everlasting?
R. I do.

Litany

205   *The minister may adapt or shorten the litany according to the condition of the sick person. The litany may be omitted if the sick person has made the profession of faith and appears to be tiring.*

My brothers and sisters, with one heart let us call on our Savior Jesus Christ.

You loved us to the very end and gave yourself over to death in order to give us life. For our brother/sister, Lord, we pray:
R. Lord, hear our prayer.

You said to us: "All who eat my flesh and drink my blood will live for ever." For our brother/sister, Lord, we pray:
R. Lord, hear our prayer.

You invite us to join in the banquet where pain and sorrow, sadness and separation will be no more. For our brother/sister, Lord, we pray:
R. Lord, hear our prayer.

LITURGY OF VIATICUM

The Lord's Prayer

206   The minister introduces the Lord's Prayer in these words:

A

Now let us offer together the prayer our Lord Jesus Christ taught us:

B

And now let us pray with confidence as Christ our Lord commanded:

All say:

Our Father . . .

Communion as Viaticum

207   The sick person and all present may receive communion under both kinds. When the minister gives communion to the sick person, the form for viaticum is used.

The minister shows the eucharistic bread to those present, saying:

A

Jesus Christ is the food for our journey;
he calls us to the heavenly table.

B

This is the bread of life.
Taste and see that the Lord is good.

The sick person and all who are to receive communion say:

Lord, I am not worthy to receive you,
but only say the word and I shall be healed.

The minister goes to the sick person and, showing the blessed sacrament, says:

The body of Christ.

The sick person answers: "Amen."

Then the minister says:

The blood of Christ.

The sick person answers: "Amen."

Immediately, or after giving communion to the sick person, the minister adds:

May the Lord Jesus Christ protect you
and lead you to eternal life.
R. *Amen.*

Others present who wish to receive communion then do so in the usual way.

After the conclusion of the rite, the minister cleanses the vessel as usual.

Silent Prayer

208   *Then a period of silence may be observed.*

Prayer after Communion

209   *The minister says the concluding prayer.*

Let us pray.

Pause for silent prayer, if this has not preceded.

A.

God of peace,
you offer eternal healing to those who believe in you;
you have refreshed your servant N.
with food and drink from heaven:
lead him/her safely into the kingdom of light.

We ask this through Christ our Lord.
R. Amen.

B

All-powerful and ever-living God,
may the body and blood of Christ your Son
be for our brother/sister N.
a lasting remedy for body and soul.

We ask this through Christ our Lord.
R. Amen.

C

Father,
your son, Jesus Christ, is our way, our truth,
        and our life.
Look with compassion on your servant N.
who has trusted in your promises.
You have refreshed him/her with the body and blood
        of your Son:
may he/she enter your kingdom in peace.

We ask this through Christ our Lord.
R. Amen.

CONCLUDING RITES

Blessing

210   A minister who is not a priest or deacon invokes God's blessing and makes the sign of the cross on himself or herself, while saying:

May the Lord bless us,
protect us from all evil,
and bring us to everlasting life.
R. Amen.

Sign of Peace

211   The minister and the others present may then give the sick person the sign of peace.

Commendation of the Dying

INTRODUCTION

Into your hands, Lord, I commend my spirit.

212   In viaticum the dying person is united with Christ in his passage out of this world to the Father. Through the prayers for the commendation of the dying contained in this chapter, the Church helps to sustain this union until it is brought to fulfillment after death.

213   Christians have the responsibility of expressing their union in Christ by joining the dying person in prayer for God's mercy and for confidence in Christ. In particular, the presence of a priest or deacon shows more clearly that the Christian dies in the communion of the Church. He should assist the dying person and those present in the recitation of the prayers of commendation and, following death, he should lead those present in the prayer after death. If the priest or deacon is unable to be present because of other serious pastoral obligations, other members of the community should be prepared to assist with these prayers and should have the texts readily available to them.

214   The minister may choose texts from among the prayers, litanies, aspirations, psalms, and readings provided in this chapter, or others may be added. In the selection of these texts the minister should keep in mind the condition and piety of both the dying person and the members of the family who are

present. The prayers are best said in a slow, quiet voice, alternating with periods of silence. If possible, the minister says one or more of the brief prayer formulas with the dying person. These may be softly repeated two or three times.

215   These texts are intended to help the dying person, if still conscious, to face the natural human anxiety about death by imitating Christ in his patient suffering and dying. The Christian will be helped to surmount his or her fear in the hope of heavenly life and resurrection through the power of Christ, who destroyed the power of death by his own dying.

Even if the dying person is not conscious, those who are present will draw consolation from these prayers and come to a better understanding of the paschal character of Christian death. This may be visibly expressed by making the sign of the cross on the forehead of the dying person, who was first signed with the cross at baptism.

216   Immediately after death has occurred, all may kneel while one of those present leads the prayers given on pp. 274–286.

SHORT TEXTS

217   One or more of the following short texts may be recited with the dying person. If necessary, they may be softly repeated two or three times.

Romans 8:35
Who can separate us from the love of Christ?

Romans 14:8
Whether we live or die, we are the Lord's.

2 Corinthians 5:1
We have an everlasting home in heaven.

1 Thessalonians 4:17
We shall be with the Lord for ever.

1 John 3:2
We shall see God as he really is.

1 John 3:14
We have passed from death to life
because we love each other.

Psalm 25:1
To you, Lord, I lift up my soul.

Psalm 27:1
The Lord is my light and my salvation.

Psalm 27:13
I believe that I shall see the goodness of the Lord
in the land of the living.

Psalm 42:3
My soul thirsts for the living God.

Psalm 23:4
Though I walk in the shadow of death,
I will fear no evil,
for you are with me.

Matthew 25:34
Come, blessed of my Father,
says the Lord Jesus,
and take possession of the kingdom
prepared for you.

Luke 23:43
The Lord Jesus says,
today you will be with me in paradise.

John 14:2
In my Father's home
there are many dwelling places,
says the Lord Jesus.

John 14:2–3
The Lord Jesus says,
I go to prepare a place for you,
and I will come again to take you to myself.

John 17:24
I desire that where I am,
they also may be with me,
says the Lord Jesus.

John 6:40
Everyone who believes in the Son
has eternal life.

Psalm 31:5a
Into your hands, Lord,
I commend my spirit.

Acts 7:59
Lord Jesus, receive my spirit.

Holy Mary, pray for me.

Saint Joseph, pray for me.

Jesus, Mary, and Joseph,
assist me in my last agony.

READING

218   *The word of God is proclaimed by one of those present or by the minister.
Selections from Part III or from the following readings may be used:*

A *Job 19:23–27a*
Job's act of faith is a model for our own; God is the God of the living.

B *Psalm 23*
C *Psalm 25*
D *Psalm 91*
E *Psalm 121*
F *1 John 4:16*

G Revelation 21:1–5a, 6–7
God our Father is the God of newness of life; it is his desire that we should come to share his life with him.

H Matthew 25:1–13
Jesus bid us be prepared for our ultimate destiny, which is eternal life.

I Luke 22:39–46
Jesus is alive to our pain and sorrow, because faithfulness to his Father's will cost him life itself.

J Luke 24:1–8
Jesus' death is witnessed by his friends.

K Luke 24:1–8
Jesus is alive' he gives us eternal life with the Father.

L John 6:37–40
Jesus will raise his own from death and give them eternal life.

M John 14:1–6, 23, 27
The love of Jesus can raise us up from the sorrow of death to the joy of eternal life.

Litany of the Saints

219   When the condition of the dying person calls for the use of brief forms of prayer, those who are present are encouraged to pray the litany of the saints — or at least some of its invocations — for him or her. Special mention may be made of the patron saints of the dying person, of the family, and of the parish. The litany may be said or sung in the usual way. Other customary prayers may also be used.

Lord, have mercy . . . . Lord, have mercy
Christ, have mercy . . . . Christ, have mercy
Lord, have mercy . . . . Lord, have mercy
Holy Mary, Mother of God . . . . pray for him/her
Holy angels of God . . . . pray for him/her
Abraham, our father in faith . . . . . pray for him/her
David, leader of God's people . . . . pray for him/her
All holy patriarchs and prophets . . pray for him/her

Saint John the Baptist . . . . pray for him/her
Saint Joseph . . . . pray for him/her
Saint Peter and Saint Paul . . . . pray for him/her
Saint Andrew . . . . pray for him/her
Saint John . . . . pray for him/her
Saint Mary Magdalene . . . . pray for him/her
Saint Stephen . . . . pray for him/her
Saint Ignatius . . . . pray for him/her
Saint Lawrence . . . . pray for him/her
Saint Perpetua and Saint Felicity . . pray for him/her
Saint Agnes . . . . pray for him/her
Saint Gregory . . . . pray for him/her
Saint Augustine . . . . pray for him/her
Saint Athanasius . . . . pray for him/her
Saint Basil . . . . pray for him/her
Saint Martin . . . . pray for him/her
Saint Benedict . . . . pray for him/her
Saint Francis and Saint Dominic . . pray for him/her
Saint Francis Xavier . . . . pray for him/her
Saint John Vianney . . . . pray for him/her
Saint Catherine . . . . pray for him/her
Saint Teresa . . . . pray for him/her

Other saints may be included here.

All holy men and women . . . . pray for him/her
Lord, be merciful . . . . Lord, save your people
From all evil . . . . Lord, save your people
From every sin . . . . Lord, save your people
From Satan's power . . . . Lord, save your people
At the moment of death . . . . Lord, save your people

From everlasting death . . . . . Lord, save your people
On the day of judgment . . . . Lord, save your people
By your coming as man . . . . Lord, save your people
By your suffering and cross . Lord, save your people
By your death
      and rising to new life . Lord, save your people
By your return in glory
      to the Father . . . . Lord, save your people
By your gift
      of the Holy Spirit . . . . Lord, save your people
By your coming again
      in glory . . . . Lord, save your people

Be merciful to us sinners . . . . Lord, hear our prayer
Bring *N.* to eternal life,
      first promised to
      him/her in baptism . . . . Lord, hear our prayer
Raise *N.* on the last day,
      for he/she has eaten
      the bread of life . . . . . . Lord, hear our prayer
Let *N.* share in your glory,
      for he/she has shared in
      your suffering and death Lord, hear our prayer
Jesus, Son of the living God . . Lord, hear our prayer

Christ, hear us . . . . Christ, hear us
Lord Jesus, hear our prayer . . . Lord, hear our prayer

B

A brief form of the litany may be prayed. Other saints may be added, including the patron saints of the dying person, of the family, and of the parish; saints to whom the dying person may have a special devotion may also be included.

Holy Mary, Mother of God . . . . pray for him/her

Holy angels of God . . . . pray for him/her

Saint John the Baptist . . . . pray for him/her

Saint Joseph . . . . pray for him/her

Saint Peter and Saint Paul . . . . pray for him/her

Other saints may be included here.

All holy men and women . . . . pray for him/her

Prayer of Commendation

220 . When the moment of death seems near, some of the following prayers may be said:

A

Go forth, Christian soul, from this world
in the name of God the almighty Father,
who created you,
in the name of Jesus Christ, Son of the living God,
who suffered for you,
in the name of the Holy Spirit,
who was poured out upon you,
go forth, faithful Christian.

May you live in peace this day,
may your home be with God in Zion,
with Mary, the virgin Mother of God,
with Joseph, and all the angels and saints.

B

I commend you, my dear brother/sister,
to almighty God,
and entrust you to your Creator.
May you return to him
who formed you from the dust of the earth.
May holy Mary, the angels, and all the saints
come to meet you as you go forth from this life.
May Christ who was crucified for you
bring you freedom and peace.
May Christ who died for you
admit you into his garden of paradise.
May Christ, the true Shepherd,
acknowledge you as one of his flock.
May he forgive all your sins,
and set you among those he has chosen.
May you see your Redeemer face to face,
and enjoy the vision of God for ever.
R. Amen.

C

Welcome your servant, Lord, into the place of salvation which because of your mercy he/she rightly hoped for.

R. *Amen,* or R. *Lord, save your people.*

Deliver your servant, Lord, from every distress.

R. *Amen,* or R. *Lord, save your people.*

Deliver your servant, Lord, as you delivered Noah from the flood.

R. *Amen,* or R. *Lord, save your people.*

Deliver your servant, Lord, as you delivered Abraham from Ur of the Chaldees.

R. *Amen,* or R. *Lord, save your people.*

Deliver your servant, Lord, as you delivered Moses from the hand of the Pharaoh.

R. *Amen,* or R. *Lord, save your people.*

Deliver your servant, Lord, as you delivered Daniel from the den of lions.

R. *Amen,* or R. *Lord, save your people.*

Deliver your servant, Lord, as you delivered the three young men from the fiery furnace.

R. *Amen,* or R. *Lord, save your people.*

Deliver your servant, Lord, as you delivered Susanna from her false accusers.

R. *Amen,* or R. *Lord, save your people.*

Deliver your servant, Lord, as you delivered David
from the attacks of Saul and Goliath.
R. Amen, or R. Lord, save your people.

Deliver your servant, Lord, as you delivered Peter
and Paul from prison.
R. Amen, or R. Lord, save your people.

Deliver your servant, Lord, through Jesus our Savior,
who suffered death for us and gave us eternal life.
R. Amen, or R. Lord, save your people.

D

Lord Jesus Christ, Savior of the world,
we pray for your servant N.,
and commend him/her to your mercy.
For his/sake you came down from heaven;
receive him/her now into the joy of your kingdom.

For though he/she has sinned,
he she/has not denied the Father, the Son,
        and the Holy Spirit,
but has believed in God
and has worshipped his/her Creator.
R. Amen.

E *The following antiphon may be said or sung:*

Hail, holy Queen, Mother of mercy,
hail, our life, our sweetness, and our hope.

To you we cry, the children of Eve;
to you we send up our sighs,
mourning and weeping in this land of exile.
Turn, then, most gracious advocate,
your eyes of mercy toward us;
lead us home at last
and show us the blessed fruit of your womb, Jesus:
O clement, O loving, O sweet Virgin Mary.

Prayer after Death

221   *When death has occurred, one or more of the following prayers may
be said:*

A

Saints of God, come to his/her aid!
Come to meet him/her, angels of the Lord!
R. *Receive his/her soul and present him/her to God the
    Most High.*

May Christ, who called you, take you to himself;
may angels lead you to Abraham's side.
R. *Receive his/her soul and present him/her to God the
    Most High.*

Give him/her eternal rest, O Lord,
and may your light shine on him/her for ever.
R. *Receive his/her soul and present him/her to God the
    Most High.*

The following prayer is added:
Let us pray.

All-powerful and merciful God,
we commend to you **N.**, your servant.
In your mercy and love,
blot out the sins he/she has committed
through human weakness.
In this world he/she has died:
let him/her live with you for ever.
We ask this through Christ our Lord.
R. *Amen.*

For the solace of those present the minister may conclude these prayers with
a simple blessing or with a symbolic gesture, for example, signing the forehead
with the sign of the cross.

B   *Psalm 130*

R. *My soul hopes in the Lord.*

Out of the depths I cry to you, O LORD;
        LORD, hear my voice!
Let your ears be attentive
        to my voice in supplication.
R. *My soul hopes in the Lord.*

I trust in the LORD,
        my soul trusts in his word.
My soul waits for the LORD
        more than sentinels wait for the dawn.
R. *My soul hopes in the Lord.*

For with the LORD is kindness,
    and with him is plenteous redemption.
And he will redeem Israel
    from all their iniquities.
R. *My soul hopes in the Lord.*

The following prayer is added:
Let us pray.
God of love, welcome into your presence
your son/daughter **N.**, whom you have
    called from this life.
Release him/her from all his/her sins,
bless him/her with eternal light and peace,
raise him/her up to live for ever with all your saints
in the glory of the resurrection.
We ask this through Christ our Lord.
R. *Amen.*

C   *Psalm 23*

R. *Lord, remember me in your kingdom.*

The LORD is my shepherd; I shall not want.
    In verdant pastures he gives me repose;
Beside restful waters he leads me;
    he refreshes my soul.
R. *Lord, remember me in your kingdom.*

He guides me in right paths
    for his name's sake.

Even though I walk in the dark valley
    I fear no evil; for you are at my side
With your rod and your staff
    that give me courage.
R. Lord, remember me in your kingdom.

You spread the table before me
    in the sight of my foes;
You anoint my head with oil;
    my cup overflows.
R. Lord, remember me in your kingdom.

Only goodness and kindness follow me
    all the days of my life;
And I shall dwell in the house of the LORD
    for years to come.
R. Lord, remember me in your kingdom.

The following prayer is added:
Let us pray.

God of mercy,
hear our prayers and be merciful
to your son/daughter **N.**,
    whom you have called from this life.
Welcome him/her into the company of your saints,
in the kingdom of light and peace.
We ask this through Christ our Lord.
R. Amen.

D

Almighty and eternal God,
hear our prayers for your son/daughter N.,
whom you have called from this life to yourself.

Grant him/her light, happiness, and peace.
Let him/her pass in safety through the gates of death,
and live for ever with all your saints
in the light you promised to Abraham
and to all his descendants in faith.

Guard him/her from all harm
and on that great day of resurrection and reward
raise him/her up with all your saints.
Pardon his/her sins
and give him/her eternal life in your kingdom.

We ask this through Christ our Lord.
R. Amen.

E

Loving and merciful God,
we entrust our brother/sister to your mercy.
You loved him/her greatly in this life:
now that he/she is freed from all its cares,
give him/her happiness and peace for ever.

The old order has passed away:
welcome him/her now into paradise
where there will be no more sorrow,

no more weeping or pain,
but only peace and joy
with Jesus, your Son,
and the Holy Spirit
for ever and ever.
R. Amen.

F

God of our destiny,
into your hands we commend our brother/sister.
We are confident that with all who have died in Christ
he/she will be raised to life on the last day
and live with Christ for ever.

[We thank you for all the blessings
you gave him/her in this life
to show your fatherly care for all of us
and the fellowship which is ours with the saints
        in Jesus Christ.]

Lord, hear our prayer:
welcome our brother/sister to paradise
and help us to comfort each other
with the assurance of our faith
until we all meet in Christ
to be with you and with our brother/sister for ever.

We ask this through Christ our Lord.
R. Amen.

Prayer for the Family and Friends

222   *The following prayer may be said:*

Let us pray.

For the family and friends

God of all consolation,
in your unending love and mercy for us
you turn the darkness of death
into the dawn of new life.
Show compassion to your people in their sorrow.

[Be our refuge and our strength
to lift us from the darkness of this grief
to the peace and light of your presence.]
Your Son, our Lord Jesus Christ,
by dying for us, conquered death
and by rising again, restored life.

May we then go forward eagerly to meet him,
and after our life on earth
be reunited with our brothers and sisters
where every tear will be wiped away.
We ask this through Christ our Lord.
R. Amen.

B   *For the deceased person and for family and friends*

Lord Jesus, our Redeemer,
you willingly gave yourself up to death
so that all people might be saved
and pass from death into new life.

Listen to our prayers,
look with love on your people
who mourn and pray for their brother/sister **N.**

Lord Jesus, holy and compassionate:
forgive **N.** his/her sins.
By dying you opened the gates of life
for those who believe in you:
do not let our brother/sister be parted from you,
but by your glorious power
give him/her light, joy, and peace in heaven
where you live for ever and ever.
R. Amen.

*For the solace of those present the minister may conclude these prayers with
a simple blessing or with a symbolic gesture, for example, signing the forehead
with the sign of the cross.*

Prayers for the Dead

INTRODUCTION

I want those you have given me to be with me where I am.

223   This chapter contains prayers for use by a minister who has been called to attend a person who is already dead. A priest is not to administer the sacraments of penance or anointing. Instead, he should pray for the dead person using these or similar prayers.

224   It may be necessary to explain to the family of the person who is dead that sacraments are celebrated for the living, not for the dead, and that the dead are effectively helped by the prayers of the living.

225   To comfort those present the minister may conclude these prayers with a simple blessing or with a symbolic gesture, for example, making the sign of the cross on the forehead. A priest or deacon may sprinkle the body with holy water.

Greeting

226   The minister greets those who are present, offering them sympathy and the consolation of faith, using the following or similar words:

A

In this moment of sorrow
the Lord is in our midst
and comforts us with his word:
Blessed are the sorrowful; they shall be consoled.

B

Praised be God, the Father of our Lord Jesus Christ,
the Father of mercies,
and the God of all consolation!
He comforts us in all our afflictions
and thus enables us to comfort those who are
      in trouble,
with the same consolation
we have received from him.

Prayer

*227   The minister then says one of the following prayers, commending the
person who has just died to God's mercy and goodness:*

Let us pray.

A

Almighty and eternal God,
hear our prayers for your son/daughter **N.**,
whom you have called from this life to yourself.
Grant him/her light, happiness, and peace.
Let him/her pass in safety through the gates
      of death,
and live for ever with all your saints
in the light you promised to Abraham
and to all his descendants in faith.
Guard him/her from all harm
and on that great day of resurrection and reward
raise him/her up with all your saints.

Pardon his/her sins
and give him/her eternal life in your kingdom.
We ask this through Christ our Lord.
R. Amen.

B

Loving and merciful God,
we entrust our brother/sister to your mercy.
You loved him/her greatly in this life:
now that he/she is freed from all its cares,
give him/her happiness and peace for ever.
The old order has passed away:
welcome him/her now into paradise
where there will be no more sorrow,
no more weeping or pain,
but only peace and joy
with Jesus, your Son,
and the Holy Spirit
for ever and ever.
R. Amen.

Reading

228   *The word of God is proclaimed by one of those present or by the minister.*
One of the following readings may be used:

A Luke 23:4 4–46
B John 11:3–7, 20–27, 33–36, 41–44

Litany

229 *Then one of those present may lead the others in praying a brief form of the litany of the saints. (The full form of the litany of the saints may be found in no. 219.) Other saints may be added, including the patron saints of the dead person, of the family, and of the parish; saints to whom the deceased person may have had a special devotion may also be included.*

Saints of God, come to his/her aid!
Come to meet him/her, angels of the Lord!

Holy Mary, Mother of God	*pray for him/her*
Saint Joseph	*pray for him/her*
Saint Peter and Saint Paul	*pray for him/her*

The following prayer is added:

God of mercy,
hear our prayers and be merciful
to your son/daughter **N.**, whom you have called
    from this life.
Welcome him/her into the company of your saints,
in the kingdom of light and peace.
We ask this through Christ our Lord.
R. Amen.

The Lord's Prayer

230 *The minister introduces the Lord's Prayer in these or similar words:*

A

With God there is mercy and fullness of redemption;
let us pray as Jesus taught us to pray:

B

Let us pray for the coming of the kingdom as Jesus taught us:

All say:

Our Father . . .

Prayer of Commendation

231   The minister then concludes with the following prayer:

Lord Jesus, our Redeemer,
you willingly gave yourself up to death
so that all people might be saved
and pass from death into a new life.
Listen to our prayers,
look with love on your people
who mourn and pray for their brother/sister **N.**

Lord Jesus, holy and compassionate:
forgive **N.** his/her sins.
By dying you opened the gates of life
for those who believe in you:
do not let our brother/sister be parted from you,
but by your glorious power
give him/her light, joy, and peace in heaven
where you live for ever and ever.
R. *Amen.*

For the solace of those present the minister may conclude these prayers with a simple blessing or with a symbolic gesture, for example, signing the forehead with the sign of the cross.

THE GOSPELS FOR SUNDAYS AND HOLY DAYS OF OBLIGATION

ADVENT

December 2, 2007

First Sunday of Advent

A reading from the holy Gospel according to Matthew
24:37–44

Jesus said to his disciples:
"As it was in the days of Noah,
    so it will be at the coming of the Son of Man.
In those days before the flood,
    they were eating and drinking,
    marrying and giving in marriage,
    up to the day that Noah entered the ark.
They did not know until the flood came
        and carried them all away.
So will it be also at the coming of the Son of Man.
Two men will be out in the field;
    one will be taken, and one will be left.
Two women will be grinding at the mill;
    one will be taken, and one will be left.
Therefore, stay awake!
For you do not know on which day your Lord
        will come.

Be sure of this: if the master of the house
   had known the hour of night when the thief
      was coming,
   he would have stayed awake
   and not let his house be broken into.
So too, you also must be prepared,
   for at an hour you do not expect, the Son of Man
      will come."

The Gospel of the Lord.

EXPLANATION OF THE READING

Advent requires two things—neither of which most of us do well. One is
waiting. The other is being quiet. Advent calls us to prayer, reflection, and
a deep yearning for the Messiah. It asks of those awaiting the coming of
Christ a willing and open heart. The season is a time for searching out
within ourselves thoughts that are not in keeping with the Christian life
and for acting in ways that will build up the Christian community.

December 8, 2007

SOLEMNITY OF THE IMMACULATE CONCEPTION OF THE BLESSED VIRGIN MARY

A reading from the holy Gospel according to Luke   *1:26–38*

The angel Gabriel was sent from God
   to a town of Galilee called Nazareth,
   to a virgin betrothed to a man named Joseph,

of the house of David,
and the virgin's name was Mary.
And coming to her, he said,
"Hail, full of grace! The Lord is with you."
But she was greatly troubled at what was said
and pondered what sort of greeting this might be.
Then the angel said to her,
"Do not be afraid, Mary,
for you have found favor with God.
Behold, you will conceive in your womb and bear
a son,
and you shall name him Jesus.
He will be great and will be called Son of the
Most High,
and the Lord God will give him the throne of David
his father,
and he will rule over the house of Jacob forever,
and of his Kingdom there will be no end."
But Mary said to the angel,
"How can this be,
since I have no relations with a man?"
And the angel said to her in reply,
"The Holy Spirit will come upon you,
and the power of the Most High will
overshadow you.
Therefore the child to be born
will be called holy, the Son of God.
And behold, Elizabeth, your relative,
has also concieved a son in her old age,

and this is the sixth month for her who was
   called barren;
   for nothing will be impossible for God."
Mary said, "Behold, I am the handmaid of the Lord.
May it be done to me according to your word."
Then the angel departed from her.

The Gospel of the Lord.

EXPLANATION OF THE READING

For the solemnity of the Immaculate Conception of the Blessed Virgin
Mary, we hear an account of one woman's courage to say "yes" to God's
infinite plan of salvation. This "yes" profoundly changed the history of
humanity. Mary's openness to trust in God is a tapestry illuminating
God's saving hand at work in unexpected places. Following in her footsteps, we are called during this sacred season to say "yes" to God's plan
being conceived in and through us.

December 9, 2007

SECOND SUNDAY OF ADVENT

A reading from the holy Gospel
according to Matthew   *3:1–12*

John the Baptist appeared, preaching in the desert
   of Judea
   and saying, "Repent, for the kingdom of heaven is
   at hand!"
It was of him that the prophet Isaiah had spoken
   when he said:

A voice of one crying out in the desert,
  Prepare the way of the Lord,
    make straight his paths.
John wore clothing made of camel's hair
  and had a leather belt around his waist.
His food was locusts and wild honey.
At that time Jerusalem, all Judea,
  and the whole region around the Jordan
  were going out to him
  and were being baptized by him in the Jordan River
  as they acknowledged their sins.

When he saw many of the Pharisees and Sadducees
  coming to his baptism, he said to them, "You
    brood of vipers!
Who warned you to flee from the coming wrath?
Produce good fruit as evidence of your repentance.
And do not presume to say to yourselves,
  'We have Abraham as our father.'
For I tell you,
  God can raise up children to Abraham from
    these stones.
Even now the ax lies at the root of the trees.
Therefore every tree that does not bear good fruit
  will be cut down and thrown into the fire.
I am baptizing you with water, for repentance,
  but the one who is coming after me is mightier
    than I.
I am not worthy to carry his sandals.

He will baptize you with the Holy Spirit and fire."
His winnowing fan is in his hand.
He will clear his threshing floor
   and gather his wheat into his barn,
   but the chaff he will burn with unquenchable fire."

The Gospel of the Lord.

EXPLANATION OF THE READING

Often we talk so much about Advent as a time of waiting and watching that we tend to forget that there is something for us to do. How are we to prepare the way of the Lord? By simply opening our hearts, welcoming in Christ. We must remove those things that hinder us from receiving Christ with joy; those things, happenings, problems that we are afraid of, those things that make us anxious and cause us to get upset. To prepare the way of the Lord means letting go and simply trusting, for Christ our Lord is coming.

December 16, 2007

THIRD SUNDAY OF ADVENT

A reading from the holy Gospel according to Matthew
11:2 – 11

When John the Baptist heard in prison of the works
   of the Christ,
   he sent his disciples to Jesus with this question,
   "Are you the one who is to come,
   or should we look for another?"
Jesus said to them in reply,
   "Go and tell John what you hear and see:
   the blind regain their sight,

the lame walk,
lepers are cleansed,
the deaf hear,
the dead are raised,
and the poor have the good news proclaimed
    to them.
And blessed is the one who takes no offense at me."

As they were going off,
    Jesus began to speak to the crowds about John,
    "What did you go out to the desert to see?
A reed swayed by the wind?
Then what did you go out to see?
Someone dressed in fine clothing?
Those who wear fine clothing are in royal palaces.
Then why did you go out? To see a prophet?
Yes, I tell you, and more than a prophet.
This is the one about whom it is written:
    Behold, I am sending my messenger ahead of you;
        he will prepare your way before you.
Amen, I say to you,
    among those born of women
    there has been none greater than John the Baptist;
    yet the least in the kingdom of heaven is greater
        than he."

The Gospel of the Lord.

EXPLANATION OF THE READING

God has revealed to John that the Messiah would finally render to unrepentant wicked Jews and Gentiles the long-awaited judgment. John announced the fulfillment in the sure words of ancient prophecies. He warned that time was so short that nothing was left to do except make ready for baptism. However, when Jesus asked for baptism, John was confused; when he objected, Jesus said enigmatically, "thus it is fitting for us to fulfill all righteousness" (Matthew 3:14–15). While John sat in prison, Jesus went about healing, forgiving, and eating with sinners, prostitutes, and tax collectors.

December 23, 2007

FOURTH SUNDAY OF ADVENT

A reading from the holy Gospel according to Matthew

This is how the birth of Jesus Christ came about.
When his mother Mary was betrothed to Joseph,
   but before they lived together,
   she was found with child through the Holy Spirit.
Joseph her husband, since he was a righteous man,
   yet unwilling to expose her to shame,
   decided to divorce her quietly.
Such was his intention when, behold,
   the angel of the Lord appeared to him in a dream
     and said,
   "Joseph, son of David,
   do not be afraid to take Mary your wife into
     your home.

For it is through the Holy Spirit
   that this child has been conceived in her.
She will bear a son and you are to name him Jesus,
   because he will save his people from their sins."
All this took place to fulfill what the Lord had said
      through the prophet:
   Behold, the virgin shall conceive and bear a son,
   and they shall name him Emmanuel,
   which means "God is with us."
When Joseph awoke,
   he did as the angel of the Lord had
      commanded him
   and took his wife into his home.

The Gospel of the Lord.

EXPLANATION OF THE READING

That Jesus was born to a virgin is not merely a miracle to gape at, but
a demanding sign of his—and his true followers'—future life on the
margins of social approval. Except for a dream sent from God, even
Joseph, that just man, would have rejected the child. Beneath the charm
of Christmas, baby Jesus stands as a "sign of contradiction" (see Luke
2:34. Faith must see past the situation in front of us and dare to venture
all on him.

CHRISTMAS

December 25, 2007

SOLEMNITY OF THE NATIVITY OF THE LORD

A reading from the holy Gospel according to Luke

2:1–14

In those days a decree went out from
    Caesar Augustus
    that the whole world should be enrolled.
This was the first enrollment,
    when Quirinius was governor of Syria.
So all went to be enrolled, each to his own town.
And Joseph too went up from Galilee from the town
    of Nazareth
    to Judea, to the city of David that is
    called Bethlehem,
    because he was of the house and family of David,
    to be enrolled with Mary, his betrothed, who was
    with child.
While they were there,
    the time came for her to have her child,
    and she gave birth to her firstborn son.

She wrapped him in swaddling clothes and laid him
    in a manger,
  because there was no room for them in the inn.

Now there were shepherds in that region living in
    the fields
  and keeping the night watch over their flock.
The angel of the Lord appeared to them
  and the glory of the Lord shone around them,
  and they were struck with great fear.
The angel said to them,
  "Do not be afraid;
  for behold, I proclaim to you good news of great joy
  that will be for all the people.
For today in the city of David
  a savior has been born for you who is Christ
    and Lord.
And this will be a sign for you:
  you will find an infant wrapped in
    swaddling clothes
  and lying in a manger."
And suddenly there was a multitude of the heavenly
    host with the angel,
  praising God and saying:
  "Glory to God in the highest
    and on earth peace to those on whom his
      favor rests."

The Gospel of the Lord.

Explanation of the Reading

Lord, your word has been fulfilled. We are now at peace, conscious of your wondrous glory that fills all of creation. Our eyes have been opened to your salvation, and we are ever amazed in your sight. Guide us, Lord. Guide us with your Light.

December 30, 2007

Feast of the Holy Family of Jesus, Mary, and Joseph

A reading from the holy Gospel according to Matthew
2:13–15, 19–23

When the magi had departed, behold,
   the angel of the Lord appeared to Joseph in
     a dream and said,
   "Rise, take the child and his mother; flee to Egypt,
   and stay there until I tell you.
Herod is going to search for the child to destroy him."
Joseph rose and took the child and his mother
     by night
   and departed for Egypt.
He stayed there until the death of Herod,
   that what the Lord had said through the prophet
     might be fulfilled,
   Out of Egypt I called my son.

When Herod had died, behold,
   the angel of the Lord appeared in a dream
   to Joseph in Egypt and said,

"Rise, take the child and his mother and
   go to the land of Israel,
for those who sought the child's life are dead."
He rose, took the child and his mother,
   and went to the land of Israel.
But when he heard that Archelaus was ruling
      over Judea
   in place of his father Herod,
   he was afraid to go back there.
And because he had been warned in a dream,
   he departed for the region of Galilee.
He went and dwelt in a town called Nazareth,
   so that what had been spoken through the
      prophets might be fulfilled,
   He shall be called a Nazorean.

The Gospel of the Lord.

EXPLANATION OF THE READING

Today's feast highlights for us that God continues to reveal himself in the everyday circumstances of our lives. For most of us, the ordinary includes some form of family. It is within this intimate circle that God is present. It is here that we will grow in wisdom and grace. It is here we learn to keep things in our hearts until God grants us understanding.

January 1, 2008

SOLEMNITY OF THE BLESSED VIRGIN MARY, MOTHER OF GOD

A reading from the holy Gospel according to Luke

The shepherds went in haste to Bethlehem
    and found Mary and Joseph,
  and the infant lying in the manger.
When they saw this,
  they made known the message
  that had been told them about this child.
All who heard it were amazed
  by what had been told them by the shepherds.
And Mary kept all these things,
  reflecting on them in her heart.
Then the shepherds returned,
  glorifying and praising God
  for all they had heard and seen,
  just as it had been told to them.

When eight days were completed for
    his circumcision,
  he was named Jesus, the name given him by
    the angel
  before he was conceived in the womb.

The Gospel of the Lord.

New Year's Day is the day of resolutions. But when we make them, we have really locked ourselves into a prison of our own will. Society tells us who we should be through advertising, movies, and endless talk shows. But what today's solemnity calls to mind is that our value, our true worth, does not come from how good we look, nor how connected we are. No one would have suspected that God's great plan would rest upon a small girl from a small village in an unassuming part of the world. But God chose Mary and her dignity comes from that choice. God has also chosen us, and that is where our true dignity comes from.

January 6, 2008

SOLEMNITY OF THE EPIPHANY OF THE LORD

A reading from the holy Gospel according to Matthew

When Jesus was born in Bethlehem of Judea,
   in the days of King Herod,
   behold, magi from the east arrived in Jerusalem,
     saying,
   "Where is the newborn king of the Jews?
We saw his star at its rising
   and have come to do him homage."
When King Herod heard this,
   he was greatly troubled,
   and all Jerusalem with him.
Assembling all the chief priests and the scribes of
     the people,

he inquired of them where the Christ was to
    be born.
They said to him, "In Bethlehem of Judea,
    for thus it has been written through the prophet:
        And you, Bethlehem, land of Judah,
            are by no means least among the rulers of Judah;
        since from you shall come a ruler,
            who is to shepherd my people Israel."
Then Herod called the magi secretly
    and ascertained from them the time of the
        star's appearance.
He sent them to Bethlehem and said,
    "Go and search diligently for the child.
When you have found him, bring me word,
    that I too may go and do him homage."
After their audience with the king they set out.
And behold, the star that they had seen at its rising
        preceded them,
    until it came and stopped over the place where the
        child was.
They were overjoyed at seeing the star,
    and on entering the house
    they saw the child with Mary his mother.
They prostrated themselves and did him homage.
Then they opened their treasures
    and offered him gifts of gold, frankincense,
        and myrrh.

And having been warned in a dream not to return
    to Herod,
  they departed for their country by another way.

The Gospel of the Lord.

EXPLANATION OF THE READING

Even before Jesus could speak for himself, a star spoke for him. Today we
hear of how even the foreign magi testified on behalf of Christ. After his
death and Resurrection, this work came to the apostles. The Church
continues the tradition; the holy saints made Christ known in each age
and place. And what about us? Have we continued the work of the work
of the Epiphany, which is to make Christ known to the world? Have we
spoken of Christ to our friends and neighbors, to our children and family,
to ourselves?

January 13, 2008

FEAST OF THE BAPTISM OF THE LORD

A reading from the holy Gospel according to Matthew   3:13–17

Jesus came from Galilee to John at the Jordan
  to be baptized by him.
John tried to prevent him, saying,
  "I need to be baptized by you,
  and yet you are coming to me?"
Jesus said to him in reply,
  "Allow it now, for thus it is fitting for us
  to fulfill all righteousness."
Then he allowed him.

After Jesus was baptized,
he came up from the water and behold,
the heavens were opened for him,
and he saw the Spirit of God descending like a dove
and coming upon him.
And a voice came from the heavens, saying,
"This is my beloved Son, with whom I am
well pleased."

The Gospel of the Lord.

EXPLANATION OF THE READING

Jesus argues with John, it is fitting that we should do it this way and so
John baptizes him. And in doing so, Jesus becomes a servant—a servant
who follows the will of his Father, who goes to those who need him. And
that is how he brought peace to the world. Mother Teresa wrote that "the
fruit of love is service." It is fitting for the Lord to be baptized because
it reminds us of our own Baptism, our own calling to holiness. Our own
Baptism means that we are called to follow the law of Christ, which is
love. And that means that we too have to become servants.

Ordinary Time I

January 20, 2008

Second Sunday in Ordinary Time

A reading from the holy Gospel according to John

1:29–34

John the Baptist saw Jesus coming toward him
   and said,
  "Behold, the Lamb of God, who takes away the sin
   of the world.
He is the one of whom I said,
  'A man is coming after me who ranks ahead of me
  because he existed before me.'
I did not know him,
  but the reason why I came baptizing with water
  was that he might be made known to Israel."
John testified further, saying,
  "I saw the Spirit come down like a dove
   from heaven
  and remain upon him.
I did not know him,
  but the one who sent me to baptize with water
   told me,

'On whomever you see the Spirit come down
   and remain,
he is the one who will baptize with the Holy Spirit.'
Now I have seen and testified that he is the Son
   of God."

The Gospel of the Lord.

EXPLANATION OF THE READING

The task of John the Baptist is to make Jesus known to Israel. He testifies to Jesus as the Lamb of God, the pre-existent one, the one upon whom the Spirit has descended, the one who will baptize with the Spirit, the one who is the Son of God. Jesus is presented as the Lamb of God who will suffer and die for the redemption of the world. In acknowledging Jesus' pre-existence, John the Baptist affirms Jesus' preeminence over him. As in the synoptic Gospels, the descent of the Spirit clearly points to Jesus as God's chosen one. Jesus' identity and mission witnessed to by John the Baptist will unfold in the rest of the Gospel. Jesus will embody what it means to be called to God's service: to live a life defined by love, a love that will embrace even death for the sake of others.

January 27, 2008

THIRD SUNDAY IN ORDINARY TIME

A reading from the holy Gospel according to Matthew   4:12–17

When Jesus heard that John had been arrested,
   he withdrew to Galilee.
He left Nazareth and went to live in Capernaum by
   the sea,
   in the region of Zebulun and Naphtali,

that what had been said through Isaiah the prophet
might be fulfilled:
> Land of Zebulun and land of Naphtali,
>> the way to the sea, beyond the Jordan,
>> Galilee of the Gentiles,
> the people who sit in darkness have seen a great light,
> on those dwelling in a land overshadowed by death
>> light has arisen.

From that time on, Jesus began to preach and say,
"Repent, for the kingdom of heaven is at hand."

The Gospel of the Lord.

Longer: Matthew 4:12–23

EXPLANATION OF THE READING

"Repent, for the kingdom of heaven is at hand" (Matthew 4:17). Tied with
these words of Christ is the story of how Peter, Andrew, James, and John
dropped everything, literally everything, to follow the Lord. And this leads
to a deeper question of what it means to repent. What couldn't we leave
behind in order to follow the Lord? What couldn't we drop, let go of, leave
behind, to follow the Lord? What ever that is, that is what we need to
repent of. But this passage is not really a demand; rather, it is an invitation
to take things on faith. We all know that when we try to control life, even
our own life, things never work out as we plan. Only when we repent of
our attachment to control can God's plans come about.

February 3, 2008

Fourth Sunday in Ordinary Time

A reading from the holy Gospel according to Matthew

5:1–12a

When Jesus saw the crowds, he went up
   the mountain,
 and after he had sat down, his disciples came
   to him.
He began to teach them, saying:
   "Blessed are the poor in spirit,
    for theirs is the kingdom of heaven.
 Blessed are they who mourn,
   for they will be comforted.
 Blessed are the meek,
   for they will inherit the land.
 Blessed are they who hunger and thirst
     for righteousness,
   for they will be satisfied.
 Blessed are the merciful,
   for they will be shown mercy.
 Blessed are the clean of heart,
   for they will see God.
 Blessed are the peacemakers,
   for they will be called children of God.
 Blessed are they who are persecuted
     for the sake of righteousness,
   for theirs is the kingdom of heaven.

Blessed are you when they insult you and
    persecute you
and utter every kind of evil against you falsely
    because of me.
Rejoice and be glad,
    for your reward will be great in heaven."

The Gospel of the Lord.

EXPLANATION OF THE READING

Moses went up a mountain and received the Law. Now Jesus teaches on
a mountain. When Moses went up the mountain, no one was allowed to
go with him; but Christ goes up the mountain and invites everyone to join
him. A new level of relationship has occurred; God has invited us closer.
And we accept this invitation by following these Beatitudes of love.

LENT

February 10, 2008

FIRST SUNDAY OF LENT

A reading from the holy Gospel according to Matthew

4:1-11

At that time Jesus was led by the Spirit into
   the desert
  to be tempted by the devil.
He fasted for forty days and forty nights,
  and afterwards he was hungry.
The tempter approached and said to him,
  "If you are the Son of God,
  command that these stones become loaves
   of bread."
He said in reply,
  "It is written:
One does not live on bread alone,
  but on every word that comes forth
  from the mouth of God."

Then the devil took him to the holy city,
  and made him stand on the parapet of the temple,
  and said to him, "If you are the Son of God,
   throw yourself down.

For it is written:

He will command his angels concerning you
and with their hands they will support you,
lest you dash your foot against a stone."

Jesus answered him,

"Again it is written,
You shall not put the Lord, your God, to the test."

Then the devil took him up to a very high mountain,
and showed him all the kingdoms of the world
in their magnificence,
and he said to him, "All these I shall give to you,
if you will prostrate yourself and worship me."

At this, Jesus said to him,

"Get away, Satan!

It is written:

The Lord, your God, shall you worship
and him alone shall you serve."

Then the devil left him and, behold,
angels came and ministered to him.

The Gospel of the Lord.

EXPLANATION OF THE READING

We enter the Lenten season signed with ashes, symbolizing the dust from which we came, our choice to turn away from sin and commitment to remain faithful to the Gospel message. The ashes call us to enter a period of repentance for 40 days and nights, confessing our sins and asking for forgiveness from the fountain of redemption, Jesus Christ. Let us place ourselves at the foot of the cross, giving alms in secret, praying behind closed doors, and fasting with joy.

February 17, 2008

SECOND SUNDAY OF LENT

A reading from the holy Gospel according to Matthew 17:1–9

Jesus took Peter, James, and John his brother,
  and led them up a high mountain by themselves.
And he was transfigured before them;
  his face shone like the sun
  and his clothes became white as light.
And behold, Moses and Elijah appeared to them,
  conversing with him.
Then Peter said to Jesus in reply,
  "Lord, it is good that we are here.
If you wish, I will make three tents here,
  one for you, one for Moses, and one for Elijah."
While he was still speaking, behold,
  a bright cloud cast a shadow over them,
  then from the cloud came a voice that said,
  "This is my beloved Son, with whom I am
    well pleased;
  listen to him."
When the disciples heard this, they fell prostrate
  and were very much afraid.
But Jesus came and touched them, saying,
  "Rise, and do not be afraid."
And when the disciples raised their eyes,
  they saw no one else but Jesus alone.

As they were coming down from the mountain,
   Jesus charged them,
   "Do not tell the vision to anyone
   until the Son of Man has been raised from
      the dead."

The Gospel of the Lord.

EXPLANATION OF THE READING

The world says follow the money and you shall be happy; fulfill your
desires and you shall find peace. But in truth this is a lie. For true
happiness can be found only by going outside of ourselves. The Christian
journey begins like Abraham's: The Lord says to Abraham, go forth from
your land, from your father's house to a land that I will show you
(cf. Genesis 12:1). That same call we all are given in the waters of
Baptism: "You have become a new creation and have clothed yourself in
Christ" (Rite of Baptism). The only way true happiness can be found is by
reaching out to others. True happiness is found in love, and love cannot
be done alone. The story of Lent is really a story about love. Out of
love for us Christ undertook a lifetime of journeying, eventually reaching
the cross.

February 24, 2008

THIRD SUNDAY OF LENT

A reading from the holy Gospel according to John
4:5–15, 19b–26, 29a, 40–42

Jesus came to a town of Samaria called Sychar,
   near the plot of land that Jacob had given to his
      son Joseph.
Jacob's well was there.

Jesus, tired from his journey, sat down there at
    the well.
It was about noon.

A woman of Samaria came to draw water.
Jesus said to her,
  "Give me a drink."
His disciples had gone into the town to buy food.
The Samaritan woman said to him,
  "How can you, a Jew, ask me, a Samaritan woman,
    for a drink?"
—For Jews use nothing in common with
    Samaritans.—
Jesus answered and said to her,
  "If you knew the gift of God
  and who is saying to you, 'Give me a drink,'
  you would have asked him
  and he would have given you living water."
The woman said to him,
  "Sir, you do not even have a bucket and the
    cistern is deep;
  where then can you get this living water?
Are you greater than our father Jacob,
  who gave us this cistern and drank from it himself
  with his children and his flocks?"
Jesus answered and said to her,
  "Everyone who drinks this water will be
    thirsty again;

but whoever drinks the water I shall give will
     never thirst;
the water I shall give will become in him
a spring of water welling up to eternal life."
The woman said to him,
     "Sir, give me this water, so that I may not be thirsty
     or have to keep coming here to draw water.

"I can see that you are a prophet.
Our ancestors worshipped on this mountain,
but you people say that the place to worship
     is Jerusalem."
Jesus said to her,
     "Believe me, woman, the hour is coming
     when you will worship the Father
     neither on this mountain nor in Jerusalem.
You people worship what you do not understand;
     we worship what we understand,
     because salvation is from the Jews.
But the hour is coming, and is now here,
     when true worshipers will worship the Father
          in Spirit and truth;
     and indeed the Father seeks such people to
          worship him.
God is Spirit, and those who worship him
     must worship in Spirit and truth."

The woman said to him,
 "I know that the Messiah is coming, the one called
  the Christ;
 when he comes, he will tell us everything."
Jesus said to her,
 "I am he, the one speaking with you."

Many of the Samaritans of that town began to
  believe in him,
When the Samaritans came to him,
 they invited him to stay with them;
 and he stayed there two days.
Many more began to believe in him because of
  his word,
 and they said to the woman,
 "We no longer believe because of your word;
 for we have heard for ourselves,
 and we know that this is truly the savior of
  the world."

The Gospel of the Lord.

Longer: John 4:5–42

EXPLANATION OF THE READING

The woman carries many burdens: female, Samaritan, many times
married, and a follower of a corrupted form of Moses' covenant. John
draws her as a colorful, outspoken spiritual seeker. A lively dialogue
develops. Jesus asks for water; she points out that he has no bucket. Jesus
talks of "living water," but she misunderstands the metaphor (a common
set-up for Jesus' teaching in this Gospel). When he probes her personal
life, she realizes Jesus is no ordinary Jew. She quickly catches on, opening

the way to a frank discussion of God and worship. When she declares her faith in the Messiah, Jesus delivers the *coup de grace*: The Messiah himself is speaking with her.

March 2, 2008

Fourth Sunday of Lent

A reading from the holy Gospel according to John
9:1, 6–9, 13–17, 34–38

As Jesus passed by he saw a man blind from birth.
He spat on the ground
   and made clay with the saliva,
   and smeared the clay on his eyes, and said to him,
   "Go wash in the Pool of Siloam"—which
     means Sent—.
So he went and washed, and came back able to see.

His neighbors and those who had seen him earlier
   as a beggar said,
  "Isn't this the one who used to sit and beg?"
Some said, "It is,"
  but others said, "No, he just looks like him."
He said, "I am."

They brought the one who was once blind to
   the Pharisees.
Now Jesus had made clay and opened his eyes on
   a sabbath.

So then the Pharisees also asked him how he was
   able to see.
He said to them,
   "He put clay on my eyes, and I washed, and now
      I can see."
So some of the Pharisees said,
   "This man is not from God,
   because he does not keep the sabbath."
But others said,
   "How can a sinful man do such signs?"
And there was a division among them.
So they said to the blind man again,
   "What do you have to say about him,
   since he opened your eyes?"
He said, "He is a prophet."

They answered and said to him,
   "You were born totally in sin,
   and are you trying to teach us?"
Then they threw him out.

When Jesus heard that they had thrown him out,
   he found him and said, "Do you believe in the Son
      of Man?"
He answered and said,
   "Who is he, sir, that I may believe in him?"
Jesus said to him,
   "You have seen him,
   the one speaking with you is he."

He said,

"I do believe, Lord," and he worshiped him.

The Gospel of the Lord.

Longer: John 9:1–41

EXPLANATION OF THE READING

This Gospel has always been read in two ways. The first way shows us a wonderful miracle of Christ, an example of the power and glory of God. At the same time, the Church has also seen a second miracle in this Gospel passage. The man born blind was not only given sight, but also the gift of faith. By putting clay on the blind man's eyes Jesus was in fact recreating those eyes, restoring them to their original purpose. The same thing happens to us in the waters of Baptism. We are recreated, restored to our original purpose, which is, like the man born blind, to allow the glory and power of God, to shine through us.

March 9, 2008

FIFTH SUNDAY OF LENT

A reading from the holy Gospel according to John   *11:3–7, 17, 20–27, 33b–45*

The sisters of Lazarus sent word to Jesus saying,

"Master, the one you love is ill."

When Jesus heard this he said,

"This illness is not to end in death,

but is for the glory of God,

that the Son of God may be glorified through it."

Now Jesus loved Martha and her sister and Lazarus.

So when he heard that he was ill,
he remained for two days in the place where
he was.
Then after this he said to his disciples,
"Let us go back to Judea."

When Jesus arrived, he found that Lazarus
had already been in the tomb for four days.
When Martha heard that Jesus was coming,
she went to meet him;
but Mary sat at home.
Martha said to Jesus,
"Lord, if you had been here,
my brother would not have died.
But even now I know that whatever you ask of God,
God will give you."
Jesus said to her,
"Your brother will rise."
Martha said to him,
"I know he will rise,
in the resurrection on the last day."
Jesus told her,
"I am the resurrection and the life;
whoever believes in me, even if he dies, will live,
and everyone who lives and believes in me will
never die.
Do you believe this?"
She said to him, "Yes, Lord.

I have come to believe that you are the Christ, the
    Son of God,
  the one who is coming into the world."

He became perturbed and deeply troubled, and said,
  "Where have you laid him?"
They said to him, "Sir, come and see."
And Jesus wept.
So the Jews said, "See how he loved him."
But some of them said,
  "Could not the one who opened the eyes of the
    blind man
  have done something so that this man would not
    have died?"

So Jesus, perturbed again, came to the tomb.
It was a cave, and a stone lay across it.
Jesus said, "Take away the stone."
Martha, the dead man's sister, said to him,
  "Lord, by now there will be a stench;
  he has been dead for four days."
Jesus said to her,
  "Did I not tell you that if you believe
  you will see the glory of God?"
So they took away the stone.
And Jesus raised his eyes and said,
  "Father, I thank you for hearing me.

I know that you always hear me;
   but because of the crowd here I have said this,
   that they may believe that you sent me."
And when he had said this,
   he cried out in a loud voice,
   "Lazarus, come out!"
The dead man came out,
   tied hand and foot with burial bands,
   and his face was wrapped in a cloth.
So Jesus said to them,
   "Untie him and let him go."

Now many of the Jews who had come to Mary
   and seen what he had done began to believe
      in him.

The Gospel of the Lord.

Longer: John 11:1–49

EXPLANATION OF THE READING

What happened to Lazarus after Jesus called him out of the tomb? After
being dead and in the grave, how can life ever return to normal? Imagine
the sense of peace that came over him. There was nothing to fear
anymore, not even death. There was only the joy of each new day. All the
worries that preoccupied him in that previous life must now appear to
him as trivial. When God loves you so much that he calls you out of the
grave, your own love must increase as well. Lazarus' heart must have
grown to the point that everyone he met was greeted as a friend. In truth,
we too have been raised from the dead, in the waters of Baptism. Therefore
we too, should live as Lazarus did, after he came out of the tomb.

Palm Sunday of the Lord's Passion

The Passion of our Lord Jesus Christ according to Matthew

27:11–54.

Jesus stood before the governor, Pontius Pilate,
   who questioned him,
  "Are you the king of the Jews?"
Jesus said, "You say so."
And when he was accused by the chief priests
   and elders,
  he made no answer.
Then Pilate said to him,
  "Do you not hear how many things they are
    testifying against you?"
But he did not answer him one word,
  so that the governor was greatly amazed.

Now on the occasion of the feast
  the governor was accustomed to release
   to the crowd
  one prisoner whom they wished.
And at that time they had a notorious prisoner
  called Barabbas.
So when they had assembled, Pilate said to them,
  "Which one do you want me to release to you,
  Barabbas, or Jesus called Christ?"

For he knew that it was out of envy
   that they had handed him over.
While he was still seated on the bench,
   his wife sent him a message,
   "Have nothing to do with that righteous man.
I suffered much in a dream today because of him."
The chief priests and the elders persuaded the crowds
   to ask for Barabbas but to destroy Jesus.
The governor said to them in reply,
   "Which of the two do you want me to release
      to you?"
They answered, "Barabbas!"
Pilate said to them,
   "Then what shall I do with Jesus called Christ?"
They all said,
   "Let him be crucified!"
But he said,
   "Why? What evil has he done?"
They only shouted the louder,
   "Let him be crucified!"
When Pilate saw that he was not succeeding at all,
   but that a riot was breaking out instead,
   he took water and washed his hands in the sight
      of the crowd,
   saying, "I am innocent of this man's blood.
Look to it yourselves."

And the whole people said in reply,
  "His blood be upon us and upon our children."
Then he released Barabbas to them,
  but after he had Jesus scourged,
  he handed him over to be crucified.

Then the soldiers of the governor took Jesus inside
    the praetorium
  and gathered the whole cohort around him.
They stripped off his clothes
  and threw a scarlet military cloak about him.
Weaving a crown out of thorns, they placed it on
    his head,
  and a reed in his right hand.
And kneeling before him, they mocked him, saying,
  "Hail, King of the Jews!"
They spat upon him and took the reed
  and kept striking him on the head,
And when they had mocked him,
  they stripped him of the cloak,
  dressed him in his own clothes,
  and led him off to crucify him.

As they were going out, they met a Cyrenian
    named Simon;
  this man they pressed into service
  to carry his cross.

And when they came to a place called Golgotha
   —which means Place of the Skull—,
   they gave Jesus wine to drink mixed gall.
But when he had tasted it, he refused to drink.
After they had crucified him,
   they divided his garments by casting lots;
   then they sat down and kept watch over him there.
And they placed over his head the written charge
      against him:
   This is Jesus, the King of the Jews.
Two revolutionaries were crucified with him,
   one on his right and the other on his left.
Those passing by reviled him, shaking their heads
      and saying,
   "You who would destroy the temple and rebuild it
      in three days,
   save yourself, if you are the Son of God,
   and come down from the cross!"
Likewise the chief priests with the scribes and elders
      mocked him and said,
   "He saved others; he cannot save himself.
So he is the king of Israel!
Let him come down from the cross now,
   and we will belief in him.
He trusted in God;
   let him deliver him now if he wants him.
For he said, 'I am the Son of God.'"
The revolutionaries who were crucified with him
   also kept abusing him in the same way.

From noon onward, darkness came over
   the whole land
  until three in the afternoon.
And about three o'clock Jesus cried out in
    a loud voice,
   "Eli, Eli, lema sabachthani?"
  which means, "My God, my God, why have you
    forsaken me?"
Some of the bystanders who heard it said,
  "This one is calling for Elijah."
Immediately one of them ran to get a sponge;
  he soaked it in wine, and putting it on a reed,
  gave it to him to drink.
But the rest said,
  "Wait, let us see if Elijah comes to save him."
But Jesus cried out again in a loud voice,
  and gave up his spirit.

Here all kneel and pause for a short time.

And behold, the veil of the sanctuary
  was torn in two from top to bottom.
The earth quaked, rocks were split, tombs
    were opened,
  and the bodies of many saints who had fallen
    asleep were raised.
And coming forth from their tombs after
    his resurrection,
  they entered the holy city and appeared to many.

The centurion and the men with him who were
    keeping watch over Jesus
feared greatly when they saw the earthquake
and all that was happening, and they said,
"Truly, this was the Son of God!"

The Gospel of the Lord.

Longer: Matthew 26:14—27:66

EXPLANATION OF THE READING

This is the day Jerusalem welcomed Jesus as a king. And yet, from this
high moment we know that we will quickly follow Christ as he is
sentenced to death as a criminal. The events of Holy Week follow closely
the words of St. Paul; from the heights of divinity and true kingship,
Christ empties himself to become a slave, accepting even death. But we
also know that this is not the end, for just as this day begins the path to
the cross, we know that it shall end with the Resurrection at Easter. Far
from being the lowest point, this week ends on the highest point ever
imagined, where we join all creation in confessing the name of Christ.

EASTER

March 23, 2008

EASTER SUNDAY: THE RESURRECTION OF THE LORD

A reading from the holy Gospel according to John

20:1–9

On the first day of the week,
   Mary of Magdala came to the tomb early in
      the morning,
   while it was still dark,
   and saw the stone removed from the tomb.
So she ran and went to Simon Peter
   and to the other disciple whom Jesus loved, and
      told them,
   "They have taken the Lord from the tomb,
   and we don't know where they put him."
So Peter and the other disciple went out and came
      to the tomb.
They both ran, but the other disciple ran faster
      than Peter
   and arrived at the tomb first;
   he bent down and saw the burial cloths there, but
      did not go in.

When Simon Peter arrived after him,
   he went into the tomb and saw the burial
     cloths there,
   and the cloth that had covered his head,
   not with the burial cloths but rolled up in
     a separate place.
Then the other disciple also went in,
   the one who had arrived at the tomb first,
   and he saw and believed.
For they did not yet understand the Scripture
   that he had to rise from the dead.

The Gospel of the Lord.

EXPLANATION OF THE READING

Jesus prayed a lament psalm on the cross, "My God, my God, why have you forsaken me?" That is the first verse of Psalm 22, the cry of a desperate sufferer who calls for God's rescue. Did God rescue Jesus? Yes, but in an unexpected way: God delivered Jesus not *from* the cross but *through* the cross in his Resurrection. In the Resurrection "the right hand of the Lord struck with power." After the disciples had time to reflect on what had happened, they would have envisioned the risen Jesus saying, "I shall not die, but live, / and declare the works of the LORD" (Psalm 118:17).

March 30, 2008

SECOND SUNDAY OF EASTER OR DIVINE MERCY SUNDAY

A reading from the holy Gospel according to John

20:19–31

On the evening of that first day of the week,
  when the doors were locked, where the
    disciples were,
  for fear of the Jews,
  Jesus came and stood in their midst
  and said to them, "Peace be with you."
When he had said this, he showed them his hands
    and his side.
The disciples rejoiced when they saw the Lord.
Jesus said to them again, "Peace be with you.
As the Father has sent me, so I send you."
And when he had said this, he breathed on them
    and said to them,
  "Receive the Holy Spirit.
Whose sins you forgive are forgiven them,
  and whose sins you retain are retained."

Thomas, called Didymus, one of the Twelve,
  was not with them when Jesus came.
So the other disciples said to him, "We have seen
    the Lord."

But he said to them,
    "Unless I see the mark of the nails in his hands
    and put my finger into the nailmarks
    and put my hand into his side, I will not believe."

Now a week later his disciples were again inside
    and Thomas was with them.
Jesus came, although the doors were locked,
    and stood in their midst and said, "Peace be
        with you."
Then he said to Thomas, "Put your finger here and
        see my hands,
    and bring your hand and put it into my side,
    and do not be unbelieving, but believe."
Thomas answered and said to him, "My Lord and
        my God!"
Jesus said to him, "Have you come to believe
        because you have seen me?
Blessed are those who have not seen and
        have believed."

Now, Jesus did many other signs in the presence of
        his disciples
    that are not written in this book.
But these are written that you may come to believe
    that Jesus is the Christ, the Son of God,
    and that through this belief you may have life in
        his name.

The Gospel of the Lord.

EXPLANATION OF THE READING

Is it really true that we have not seen? Is it really true that we have faith without having seen Christ? Is it not more truthful to say we have seen Christ? Haven't we seen Christ in others? How have we come to the faith if it wasn't that we saw Christ in others: in the stories of the saints, in the saintly lives of others in our own times, in the love and devotion of our parents, in the kindness and patience of a friend, in the gentle holiness of a grandparent? We come to believe because, in truth, we have seen Christ. And there lies the challenge; we need to be the ones of great faith so that others who see us will see Christ and believe!

April 6, 2008

THIRD SUNDAY OF EASTER

A reading from the holy Gospel according to Luke

24:13–35

That very day, the first day of the week,
    two of Jesus' disciples were going
    to a village seven miles from Jerusalem
        called Emmaus,
    and they were conversing about all the things
        that had occurred.
And it happened that while they were conversing
        and debating,
    Jesus himself drew near and walked with them,
    but their eyes were prevented from
        recognizing him.
He asked them,
    "What are you discussing as you walk along?"
They stopped, looking downcast.

One of them, named Cleopas, said to him in reply,
    "Are you the only visitor to Jerusalem
    who does not know of the things
    that have taken place there in these days?"

And he replied to them, "What sort of things?"
They said to him,
    "The things that happened to Jesus the Nazarene,
    who was a prophet mighty in deed and word
    before God and all the people,
    how our chief priests and rulers both handed
        him over
    to a sentence of death and crucified him.
But we were hoping that he would be the one to
        redeem Israel;
    and besides all this,
    it is now the third day since this took place.
Some women from our group, however, have
        astounded us:
    they were at the tomb early in the morning
    and did not find his body;
    they came back and reported
    that they had indeed seen a vision of angels
    who announced that he was alive.
Then some of those with us went to the tomb
    and found things just as the women had described,
    but him they did not see."
And he said to them, "Oh, how foolish you are!

How slow of heart to believe all that the
     prophets spoke!
Was it not necessary that the Christ should suffer
     these things
   and enter into his glory?"
Then beginning with Moses and all the prophets,
   he interpreted to them what referred to him
   in all the Scriptures.
As they approached the village to which they
     were going,
   he gave the impression that he was going
     on farther.
But they urged him, "Stay with us,
   for it is nearly evening and the day is almost over."
So he went in to stay with them.

And it happened that, while he was with them
     at table,
   he took bread, said the blessing,
   broke it, and gave it to them.
With that their eyes were opened and they
     recognized him,
   but he vanished from their sight.
Then they said to each other,
   "Were not our hearts burning within us
   while he spoke to us on the way and opened the
     Scriptures to us?"
So they set out at once and returned to Jerusalem
   where they found gathered together

the eleven and those with them who were saying,
  "The Lord has truly been raised and has appeared
    to Simon!"
Then the two recounted
  what had taken place on the way
  and how he was made known to them in the
    breaking of bread.

The Gospel of the Lord.

EXPLANATION OF THE READING

In 1513, Ponce de Leon came to the New World looking for the fountain of youth. He spent several months exploring Florida in search of this magical elixir. Of course, he never found it. As silly as this legend sounds, it rings true in most of us. We might not search for a fountain of youth, but we all hunger for a happier time, a time when our hearts were burning. The irony is that the answer to Ponce de Leon's search was in the very name he gave to the land of Florida, Pascua Florida, the flowery Passover, the day of the Resurrection. It is the Easter event that completes our joy.

April 13, 2008

FOURTH SUNDAY OF EASTER

A reading from the holy Gospel according to John   *10:1–10*

Jesus said:
"Amen, amen, I say to you,
  whoever does not enter a sheepfold through
    the gate
  but climbs over elsewhere is a thief and a robber.

But whoever enters through the gate is the shepherd
of the sheep.
The gatekeeper opens it for him, and the sheep hear
his voice,
as the shepherd calls his own sheep by name
and leads them out.
When he has driven out all his own,
he walks ahead of them, and the sheep follow him,
because they recognize his voice.
But they will not follow a stranger;
they will run away from him,
because they do not recognize the voice
of strangers."
Although Jesus used this figure of speech,
the Pharisees did not realize what he was trying to
tell them.

So Jesus said again, "Amen, amen, I say to you,
I am the gate for the sheep.
All who came before me are thieves and robbers,
but the sheep did not listen to them.
I am the gate.
Whoever enters through me will be saved,
and will come in and go out and find pasture.
A thief comes only to steal and slaughter and destroy;
I came so that they might have life
and have it more abundantly."

The Gospel of the Lord.

EXPLANATION OF THE READING

One of the oldest Christian images is of a man, the Savior, carrying a sheep on his shoulders. It is the image of the Good Shepherd. Jesus is the one that the twenty-third Psalm speaks of, in perhaps the most beautiful poem ever written: The Lord is my Shepherd. Christ has walked through that dark valley with courage and faith in his Father. And He made it through, to the other side; that is the Resurrection! And what is of great importance to us is that he has promised to walk with us with his rod and his staff in his hands. How can we be so sure? How can we actually see him standing there by our side with that rod and with that staff? All we need to do is to look at the cross, for his rod and his staff are there, the two components that create the cross: the rod is the horizontal beam and the staff is the vertical pole of the cross.

April 20, 2008

FIFTH SUNDAY OF EASTER

A reading from the holy Gospel according to John   14:1–12

Jesus said to his disciples:
   "Do not let your hearts be troubled.
You have faith in God; have faith also in me.
In my Father's house there are many dwelling places.
If there were not,
      would I have told you that I am going to prepare
         a place for you?
And if I go and prepare a place for you,
   I will come back again and take you to myself,
      so that where I am you also may be.
Where I am going you know the way."

Thomas said to him,
  "Master, we do not know where you are going;
  how can we know the way?"

Jesus said to him, "I am the way and the truth and
    the life.
No one comes to the Father except through me.
If you know me, then you will also know my Father.
From now on you do know him and have seen him."
Philip said to him,
  "Master, show us the Father, and that will be
    enough for us."
Jesus said to him, "Have I been with you for so long
    a time
  and you still do not know me, Philip?
Whoever has seen me has seen the Father.
How can you say, 'Show us the Father'?
Do you not believe that I am in the Father
    and the Father is in me?
The words that I speak to you I do not speak on
    my own.
The Father who dwells in me is doing his works.
Believe me that I am in the Father and the Father is
    in me,
  or else, believe because of the works themselves.

Amen, amen, I say to you,
   whoever believes in me will do the works that I do,
   and will do greater ones than these,
   because I am going to the Father."

The Gospel of the Lord.

EXPLANATION OF THE READING

Sometimes our culture seems to be based, fundamentally, on the notion of tragedy. Western culture thrives on tragedy, tension, and conflict. What sells newspapers? Tragedy. What is always reported on the nightly news? Tragedy. Sometimes we see Christ's story as an ancient and classic tragedy; we see the struggle he went through, we talk about his cross, and his death. At times we fail to see that Christ's death and Resurrection are not about the distant past but about our lives here and now. Christ's death and resurrection offer to the world an alternative to the cycle of sin, of violence and death. Christ overcame all that not by fighting it, nor by controlling it, but by radically resisting it through love. That is the way we should follow.

April 27, 2008

SIXTH SUNDAY OF EASTER

A reading from the holy Gospel according to John
14:15–21

Jesus said to his disciples:
"If you love me, you will keep my commandments.
And I will ask the Father,
   and he will give you another Advocate to be with
      you always,

the Spirit of truth, whom the world cannot accept,
  because it neither sees nor knows him.
But you know him, because he remains with you,
  and will be in you.
I will not leave you orphans; I will come to you.
In a little while the world will no longer see me,
  but you will see me, because I live and you will live.
On that day you will realize that I am in my Father
  and you are in me and I in you.
Whoever has my commandments and observes them
  is the one who loves me.
And whoever loves me will be loved by my Father,
  and I will love him and reveal myself to him."

The Gospel of the Lord.

EXPLANATION OF THE READING

Christ always seems to point us in the other direction: whatever it is
you are thinking of doing, do the opposite and you will be all right.
Whatever you think is happening, think the opposite and you will get it
right. Here Christ seems to be saying, "If you think you know what love is
all about, think again. You see love as the fulfillment of happiness. But
think again. True love means sacrifice; true love means being willing to let
go of everything, even your life for the sake of the other." It is the same
love that Christ demonstrates as he hangs on the cross. Christ commands
us to think differently, to think contrary to the ways of the world, and to
think with true hearts. What is ironic about all this is that we think that if
we sacrifice some of our pleasures and desires, we will never be happy,
we will never have our own needs met. But as Christ always says,
think again.

May 1, 2008

SOLEMNITY OF THE ASCENSION OF THE LORD

A reading from the holy Gospel according to Matthew
28:16–20

The eleven disciples went to Galilee,
  to the mountain to which Jesus had ordered them.
When they saw him, they worshiped, but
    they doubted.
Then Jesus approached and said to them,
  "All power in heaven and on earth has been given
    to me.
Go, therefore, and make disciples of all nations,
  baptizing them in the name of the Father,
  and of the Son, and of the Holy Spirit,
  teaching them to observe all that I have
    commanded you.
And behold, I am with you always, until the end of
    the age."

The Gospel of the Lord.

EXPLANATION OF THE READING

Today's solemnity is more about the ending of Jesus' earthly ministry than it is about where Jesus has gone. The Gospel focuses upon the disciples—upon us. We are to be witnesses, those who offer testimony, to the forgiveness of sins accomplished in Christ Jesus. We are not to work on our own; we have been promised power from on high. Great things have been asked of us and even greater things have been promised.

May 4, 2008

Seventh Sunday of Easter

A reading from the holy Gospel according to John

17:1–11a

Jesus raised his eyes to heaven and said,
"Father, the hour has come.
Give glory to your son, so that your son may
    glorify you,
    just as you gave him authority over all people,
    so that your son may give eternal life to all you
    gave him.
Now this is eternal life,
    that they should know you, the only true God,
    and the one whom you sent, Jesus Christ.
I glorified you on earth
    by accomplishing the work that you gave me to do.
Now glorify me, Father, with you,
    with the glory that I had with you before the
    world began.

"I revealed your name to those whom you gave me
    out of the world.
They belonged to you, and you gave them to me,
    and they have kept your word.
Now they know that everything you gave me is
    from you,

because the words you gave to me I have given
to them,
and they accepted them and truly understood
that I came from you,
and they have believed that you sent me.
I pray for them.
I do not pray for the world but for the ones you have
given me,
because they are yours, and everything of mine
is yours
and everything of yours is mine,
and I have been glorified in them.
And now I will no longer be in the world,
but they are in the world, while I am coming
to you."

The Gospel of the Lord.

EXPLANATION OF THE READING

By this point in the Gospel, Jesus has been betrayed and likely
disappointed to an unimaginable degree, and his Passion will begin soon.
He is near the cross, yet he speaks of glorification. The cross and the
Resurrection are so close in the theology of the Gospel according to John
that Jesus' prayer just before his Passion is about glorification. The
Paschal Mystery is not a theology of death displaced by Resurrection, but
of death *and* Resurrection. Today's reading reflects this mystery of faith
and the compassion of Jesus.

May 11, 2008

Solemnity of Pentecost

A reading from the holy Gospel according to John

20:19–23

On the evening of that first day of the week,
  when the doors were locked, where the
    disciples were,
  for fear of the Jews,
  Jesus came and stood in their midst
  and said to them, "Peace be with you."
When he had said this, he showed them his hands
  and his side.
The disciples rejoiced when they saw the Lord.
Jesus said to them again, "Peace be with you.
As the Father has sent me, so I send you."
And when he had said this, he breathed on them
  and said to them,
  "Receive the Holy Spirit.
Whose sins you forgive are forgiven them,
  and whose sins you retain are retained."

The Gospel of the Lord.

EXPLANATION OF THE READING

A long time ago, a small band of nomads wandered the desert after
escaping slavery in Egypt. They were united together by tradition, by
blood, and especially by God under the law given to them through Moses.
Over time, the people remembered the gifts the Lord had given them:
freedom, security, and the harvest. And so each year, they set aside a day
of celebration to give thanks, called Pentecost. After Christ's ascension,

a crowd formed in Jerusalem. In no way was this crowd united; they came from all over and spoke different languages. Yet through the Holy Spirit, they heard one simple message: the mighty work of God though his Son Jesus Christ. No longer do we simply celebrate the harvest, but we rejoice in being overwhelmed by the gifts of the Holy Spirit.

ORDINARY TIME II

May 18, 2008

SOLEMNITY OF THE MOST HOLY TRINITY

A reading from the holy Gospel according to John   *3:16–18*

God so loved the world that he gave his only Son,
  so that everyone who believes in him might
    not perish
  but might have eternal life.
For God did not send his Son into the world
    to condemn the world,
  but that the world might be saved through him.
Whoever believes in him will not be condemned,
  but whoever does not believe has already been
    condemned,
  because he has not believed in the name of the
    only Son of God.

The Gospel of the Lord.

EXPLANATION OF THE READING

The Emperor called for a debate on religion. Pope Sylvester was the only Christian present. Soon, all of the scholars ganged up on the Pope. What upset them was that the Pope won each argument with a simple, easy to understand proof. Frustrated, the scholars conferred with each other;

they came back and asked Sylvester, "How can you say that your Christian faith makes sense when you believe in one God, but are always talking about three, the Father, Son, and Holy Spirit? Unfazed, Sylvester took a cape and folded it into three folds. He then asked: "how many folds are there in this cape?" They answered, "Three." Then he asked, "How many capes, then, are there?" They had to say, "Only one." Sylvester said, "Just as there were three folds in this one cape, so there are three persons in the One God. You see my friends we worship one God, but we do not think of him as being so alone that he does not have the joy of having a son." At the heart of God there is a community of persons within one nature. And that relationship within the Holy Trinity is so strong, so powerful that it reaches out to us.

May 25, 2008

Solemnity of the Most Holy Body and Blood of Christ

A reading from the holy Gospel according to John

6:51–58

Jesus said to the Jewish crowds:
"I am the living bread that came down
   from heaven;
whoever eats this bread will live forever;
and the bread that I will give
is my flesh for the life of the world."

The Jews quarreled among themselves, saying,
"How can this man give us his flesh to eat?"
Jesus said to them,
"Amen, amen, I say to you,

unless you eat the flesh of the Son of Man and
   drink his blood,
you do not have life within you.
Whoever eats my flesh and drinks my blood
   has eternal life,
   and I will raise him on the last day.
For my flesh is true food,
   and my blood is true drink.
Whoever eats my flesh and drinks my blood
   remains in me and I in him.
Just as the living Father sent me
   and I have life because of the Father,
   so also the one who feeds on me
   will have life because of me.
This is the bread that came down from heaven.
Unlike your ancestors who ate and still died,
   whoever eats this bread will live forever."

The Gospel of the Lord.

EXPLANATION OF THE READING

The Eucharist gives us Christ's presence, and it also gives us Jesus
Christ's unifying love for his community to imitate. His body and blood
re-inscribe his story and his character within us. We receive his benefits,
and also are formed to live as he lived. His love infuses us not with
a formless euphoria, but with a purposeful energy that acts in scripturally
identifiable expressions of love to others.

June 1, 2008

NINTH SUNDAY IN ORDINARY TIME

A reading from the holy Gospel according to Matthew 7:21–27

Jesus said to his disciples:
"Not everyone who says to me, 'Lord, Lord,'
    will enter the kingdom of heaven,
    but only the one who does the will of my Father
        in heaven.
Many will say to me on that day,
    'Lord, Lord, did we not prophesy in your name?
Did we not drive out demons in your name?
Did we not do mighty deeds in your name?'
Then I will declare to them solemnly,
    'I never knew you. Depart from me, you evildoers.'

"Everyone who listens to these words of mine and
        acts on them
    will be like a wise man who built his house on rock.
The rain fell, the floods came,
    and the winds blew and buffeted the house.
But it did not collapse; it had been set solidly on rock.
And everyone who listens to these words of mine
    but does not act on them
    will be like a fool who built his house on sand.

The rain fell, the floods came,
and the winds blew and buffeted the house.
And it collapsed and was completely ruined."

The Gospel of the Lord.

EXPLANATION OF THE READING

These words come at the end of Jesus' Sermon on the Mount, where he
not only gives the Beatitudes, but a series of precepts ranging from the
role of the disciple to anger, adultery, and lust. These teachings of Christ
are the bricks he wants us to use to build a firm foundation.

June 8, 2008

TENTH SUNDAY IN ORDINARY TIME

A reading from the holy Gospel
according to Matthew   9:9–13

As Jesus passed on from there,
he saw a man named Matthew sitting at the
customs post.
He said to him, "Follow me."
And he got up and followed him.
While he was at table in his house,
many tax collectors and sinners came
and sat with Jesus and his disciples.
The Pharisees saw this and said to his disciples,
"Why does your teacher eat with tax collectors
and sinners?"

He heard this and said,

"Those who are well do not need a physician, but
the sick do.

Go and learn the meaning of the words,

'I desire mercy, not sacrifice.'

I did not come to call the righteous but sinners."

The Gospel of the Lord.

EXPLANATION OF THE READING

Jesus has come to proclaim the Good News of the kingdom, but he
requires workers to assist him in this task. He summons the Twelve, who
will be sent out to carry on his proclamation that the kingdom is at hand.
Jesus gives the Twelve authority over demons and illness. In today's
Gospel their authority is confined to "lost sheep of the house of Israel"
(Matthew 10:5–6), but at the end of the Gospel they will be commissioned to go forth to all nations (Matthew 28:19–20).

June 15, 2008

ELEVENTH SUNDAY IN ORDINARY TIME

A reading from the holy Gospel
according to Matthew   9:36—10:8

At the sight of the crowds, Jesus' heart was moved
        with pity for them
    because they were troubled and abandoned,
    like sheep without a shepherd.
Then he said to his disciples,
    "The harvest is abundant but the laborers are few;
    so ask the master of the harvest
    to send out laborers for his harvest."

Then he summoned his twelve disciples
   and gave them authority over unclean spirits
   to drive them out and to cure every disease and
      every illness.
The names of the twelve apostles are these:
   first, Simon called Peter, and his brother Andrew;
   James, the son of Zebedee, and his brother John;
   Philip and Bartholomew, Thomas and Matthew
      the tax collector;
   James, the son of Alphaeus, and Thaddeus;
   Simon from Cana, and Judas Iscariot who
      betrayed him.

Jesus sent out these twelve after instructing
      them thus,
   "Do not go into pagan territory or enter
      a Samaritan town.
Go rather to the lost sheep of the house of Israel.
As you go, make this proclamation:
   'The kingdom of heaven is at hand.'
Cure the sick, raise the dead, cleanse lepers, drive
      out demons.
Without cost you have received; without cost you
      are to give."

The Gospel of the Lord.

EXPLANATION OF THE READING

Here is Jesus telling the twelve to go out and proclaim that the kingdom
of heaven is at hand, to cure the sick, to raise the dead, to cleanse the
lepers, and to drive out demons. To say the least this list of objectives

seems a little daunting, and we say to ourselves, "thank God I am not an apostle." By the grace of Baptism, however, we become members of the priesthood of believers, and that means that this long list of chores Jesus gives is also part of our job description! As part of the priesthood of all the baptized, our role is to be Christ to the whole world; to go out there and preach the Good News, to live a good and holy life that inspires others to follow Christ. God wants us to help him, to be his instruments in the world.

June 22, 2008

TWELFTH SUNDAY IN ORDINARY TIME

A reading from the holy Gospel according to Matthew
10:26–33

Jesus said to the Twelve:
"Fear no one.
Nothing is concealed that will not be revealed,
   nor secret that will not be known.
What I say to you in the darkness, speak in the light;
   what you hear whispered, proclaim on
      the housetops.
And do not be afraid of those who kill the body
      but cannot kill the soul;
   rather, be afraid of the one who can destroy
   both soul and body in Gehenna.
Are not two sparrows sold for a small coin?
Yet not one of them falls to the ground
   without your Father's knowledge.
Even all the hairs of your head are counted.

So do not be afraid; you are worth more than
  many sparrows.
Everyone who acknowledges me before others
  I will acknowledge before my heavenly Father.
But whoever denies me before others,
  I will deny before my heavenly Father."

The Gospel of the Lord.

EXPLANATION OF THE READING

Remember the story of Adam and Eve in the Garden? After they ate from
the tree, from which they were not supposed to eat, their eyes were
opened and they realized that they were naked. And so, they made
clothes for themselves. As soon as God returned to the garden he knew
something was up. They thought they could hide from the Lord, but with
God there are no secrets. Today, part of the problem is that we have been
told that guilt is a bad thing. In some cases this is true, but the advice to
simply stop feeling guilty about everything and anything we do has
become a really a big problem. What we have done is we have hidden
from ourselves the fact that we have sinned. Guilt is the pricking of our
conscience, telling us that something is wrong. The solution is not to
simply get rid of the guilt, but to find the source for that guilt.

June 29, 2008

SOLEMNITY OF SAINT PETER AND SAINT PAUL, APOSTLES

A reading from the holy Gospel according to Matthew

16:13–19

When Jesus went into the region of Caesarea Philippi
  he asked his disciples,
    "Who do people say that the Son of Man is?"

They replied, "Some say John the Baptist,
    others Elijah,
  still others Jeremiah or one of the prophets."
He said to them, "But who do you say that I am?"
Simon Peter said in reply,
  "You are the Christ, the Son of the living God."
Jesus said to him in reply, "Blessed are you, Simon
    son of Jonah.
For flesh and blood has not revealed this to you,
    but my heavenly Father.
And so I say to you, you are Peter,
  and upon this rock I will build my Church,
  and the gates of the netherworld shall not prevail
    against it.
I will give you the keys to the Kingdom of heaven.
Whatever you bind on earth shall be bound
    in heaven;
  and whatever you loose on earth shall be loosed
    in heaven."

The Gospel of the Lord.

EXPLANATION OF THE READING

Why does the Church link these two saints together on this day? Each
certainly deserves his own day, which they have; so why are they
together on this solemnity? The Church answers this in the Prayer after
Communion: "by [their] teaching . . . keep us united in your love." Any
gift of authority or teaching that was given to them was for the single
purpose of promoting the Good News. Anything else was simply a dis-
traction to this mission, even differences of personality or temperament.
In these two saints we see one of the marks of the Church, the Church
as one.

July 6, 2008

Fourteenth Sunday in Ordinary Time

A reading from the holy Gospel according to Matthew

11:25–30

At that time Jesus exclaimed:
"I give praise to you, Father, Lord of heaven
    and earth,
   for although you have hidden these things
   from the wise and the learned
   you have revealed them to little ones.
Yes, Father, such has been your gracious will.
All things have been handed over to me by my Father.
No one knows the Son except the Father,
   and no one knows the Father except the Son
   and anyone to whom the Son wishes to reveal him.

"Come to me, all you who labor and are burdened,
   and I will give you rest.
Take my yoke upon you and learn from me,
   for I am meek and humble of heart;
   and you will find rest for yourselves.
For my yoke is easy, and my burden light."

The Gospel of the Lord.

Explanation of the Reading

Matthew wrote his Gospel in turbulent times, just after the revolt against
the Romans that ended in the destruction of the Temple, forty years after

Jesus' death. He was writing for Jewish converts to Christ—people who had obeyed the "yoke of the law" as taught by the Pharisees in its strictest form. Often this yoke was impossible to bear; a host of precise rules and restrictions made salvation seem very far away. Matthew assures them, and us, that Christ's yoke is easy and his burden light.

July 13, 2008

FIFTEENTH SUNDAY IN ORDINARY TIME

A reading from the holy Gospel according to Matthew 13:1–9

On that day, Jesus went out of the house and sat
    down by the sea.
Such large crowds gathered around him
    that he got into a boat and sat down,
    and the whole crowd stood along the shore.
And he spoke to them at length in parables, saying:
    "A sower went out to sow.
And as he sowed, some seed fell on the path,
    and birds came and ate it up.
Some fell on rocky ground, where it had little soil.
It sprang up at once because the soil was not deep,
    and when the sun rose it was scorched,
    and it withered for lack of roots.
Some seed fell among thorns, and the thorns grew up
    and choked it.

But some seed fell on rich soil, and produced fruit,
   a hundred or sixty or thirtyfold.
Whoever has ears ought to hear."

The Gospel of the Lord.

Longer: Matthew 13:1–23

EXPLANATION OF THE READING

Like the seed sown among thorns, we can be distracted and weakened
by anxieties or comforts. Jesus is single-minded, not distracted by worries
or dependent on comforts, so he can resist the temptation to create food
for himself. He is content to trust in God's plan for his care.

July 20, 2008

SIXTEENTH SUNDAY IN ORDINARY TIME

A reading from the holy Gospel according to Matthew   13:24–30

Jesus proposed another parable to the crowds,
   saying:
"The kingdom of heaven may be likened to a man
   who sowed good seed in his field.
While everyone was asleep his enemy came
   and sowed weeds all through the wheat, and then
   went off.
When the crop grew and bore fruit, the weeds
   appeared as well.

The slaves of the householder came to him and said,
   'Master, did you not sow good seed in your field?
Where have the weeds come from?'
He answered, 'An enemy has done this.'
His slaves said to him, 'Do you want us to go and
      pull them up?'
He replied, 'No, if you pull up the weeds
   you might uproot the wheat along with them.
Let them grow together until harvest;
   then at harvest time I will say to the harvesters,
   "First collect the weeds and tie them in bundles
      for burning;
   but gather the wheat into my barn."'"

The Gospel of the Lord.

Longer: Matthew 13:24–43

EXPLANATION OF THE READING

Today's Gospel reading includes Jesus' explanation of the parable of the wheat and weeds, in which the servants want to pull the weeds but their master restrains them so that the good will not be destroyed with the bad. They are told to leave the weeds until the harvest, when all will be sorted out.

We who count ourselves disciples may think we can distinguish the wheat from the weeds, but do we not often make mistakes about people? If we root out those we think are bad, we might be destroying good wheat! Time will tell who is wheat and who is not!

July 27, 2008

SEVENTEENTH SUNDAY IN ORDINARY TIME

A reading from the holy Gospel according to Matthew   *13:44–46*

Jesus said to his disciples:
"The kingdom of heaven is like a treasure buried in
    a field,
  which a person finds and hides again,
  and out of joy goes and sells all that he has and
    buys that field.
Again, the kingdom of heaven is like a merchant
  searching for fine pearls.
When he finds a pearl of great price,
  he goes and sells all that he has and buys it.

The Gospel of the Lord.

Longer: Matthew 13:44–52

EXPLANATION OF THE READING

The kingdom of God has the power to grow from something tiny, like
a mustard seed, into something very large, a bush. The kingdom can
infuse and transform, like the yeast leavening a batch of dough. Now
we and the disciples learn about the great value of the kingdom. It is like
a treasure hidden in a field or a pearl of great price for which seekers
offer all that they have.

August 3, 2008

EIGHTEENTH SUNDAY IN ORDINARY TIME

A reading from the holy Gospel according to Matthew

14:13-21

When Jesus heard of the death of John the Baptist,
   he withdrew in a boat to a deserted place
     by himself.
The crowds heard of this and followed him on foot
   from their towns.
When he disembarked and saw the vast crowd,
   his heart was moved with pity for them,
     and he cured their sick.
When it was evening, the disciples approached him
    and said,
   "This is a deserted place and it is already late;
   dismiss the crowds so that they can go to
     the villages
   and buy food for themselves."
Jesus said to them, "There is no need for them to
    go away;
   give them some food yourselves."
But they said to him,
   "Five loaves and two fish are all we have here."
Then he said, "Bring them here to me,"
   and he ordered the crowds to sit down on
     the grass.

Taking the five loaves and the two fish, and looking
    up to heaven,
  he said the blessing, broke the loaves,
  and gave them to the disciples,
  who in turn gave them to the crowds.
They all ate and were satisfied,
  and they picked up the fragments left over —
  twelve wicker baskets full.
Those who ate were about five thousand men,
  not counting women and children.

The Gospel of the Lord.

EXPLANATION OF THE READING

St. Paul cries out, "What will separate us from the love of Christ?"
(Romans 8:35). The miracle of the loaves and the fishes, the miracle of
Jesus feeding the five thousand, is the miracle that we celebrate each and
every time we come to the altar. It is the Eucharist which makes it
impossible for us to ever be separated from the love of God. When we
receive the Eucharist we are changed for good, we are changed forever,
we are changed for the better. God himself interpenetrates our very being,
becoming so united with us that we cannot be separated from Him, not
even when we die.

August 10, 2008

Nineteenth Sunday in Ordinary Time

A reading from the holy Gospel according to Matthew

14:22–33

After he had fed the people, Jesus made the disciples
    get into a boat
  and precede him to the other side,
  while he dismissed the crowds.
After doing so, he went up on the mountain by
    himself to pray.
When it was evening he was there alone.
Meanwhile the boat, already a few miles offshore,
  was being tossed about by the waves,
    for the wind was against it.
During the fourth watch of the night,
  he came toward them walking on the sea.
When the disciples saw him walking on the sea
    they were terrified.
"It is a ghost," they said, and they cried out in fear.
At once Jesus spoke to them, "Take courage, it is I;
    do not be afraid."
Peter said to him in reply,
  "Lord, if it is you, command me to come to you on
    the water."
He said, "Come."

Peter got out of the boat and began to walk on the
    water toward Jesus.
But when he saw how strong the wind was
    he became frightened;
  and, beginning to sink, he cried out, "Lord,
    save me!"
Immediately Jesus stretched out his hand and
    caught Peter,
  and said to him, "O you of little faith, why did
    you doubt?"
After they got into the boat, the wind died down.
Those who were in the boat did him homage,
    saying,
  "Truly, you are the Son of God."

The Gospel of the Lord.

EXPLANATION OF THE READING

In the Old Testament, there are a few instances where God is described
as walking on water, as in Job, where God is described as the one who
spread out the heavens and trod on the back of the sea. These instances
connect Jesus to God, allowing his divinity to stand out. Is it any wonder
he rebukes Peter for his doubt? What we tend to forget is that after he is
pulled up, Peter, we assume, walked behind Jesus, following his footsteps
without a problem. It was only after they were back in the boat that the
wind calmed down. This shows us the way we are to live; walking in
Christ's path is the safest way.

August 15, 2008

Solemnity of the Assumption of the Blessed Virgin Mary

A reading from the holy Gospel according to Luke

1:39–56

Mary set out
    and traveled to the hill country in haste
    to a town of Judah,
    where she entered the house of Zechariah
    and greeted Elizabeth.
When Elizabeth heard Mary's greeting,
    the infant leaped in her womb,
    and Elizabeth, filled with the Holy Spirit,
    cried out in a loud voice and said,
    "Blessed are you among women,
    and blessed is the fruit of your womb.
And how does this happen to me,
    that the mother of my Lord should come to me?
For at the moment the sound of your greeting
        reached my ears,
    the infant in my womb leaped for joy.
Blessed are you who believed
    that what was spoken to you by the Lord
    would be fulfilled."

And Mary said:
    "My soul proclaims the greatness of the Lord;

my spirit rejoices in God my Savior
 for he has looked upon his lowly servant.
From this day all generations will call me blessed:
 the Almighty has done great things for me,
 and holy is his Name.
He has mercy on those who fear him
 in every generation.
He has shown the strength of his arm,
 and has scattered the proud in their conceit.
He has cast down the mighty from their thrones,
 and has lifted up the lowly.
He has filled the hungry with good things,
 and the rich he has sent away empty.
He has come to the help of his servant Israel
 for he has remembered his promise of mercy,
 the promise he made to our fathers,
 to Abraham and his children for ever."

Mary remained with her about three months
 and then returned to her home.

The Gospel of the Lord.

EXPLANATION OF THE READING

In the Book of Revelation, St. John has a vision where the beast is poised to devour the child who is in the womb of the woman who shines like the sun. It is, of course, the final battle between good and evil. This battle between good and evil is present in each of our lives. Evil usually comes to us in the form of self-centeredness. But we have to take our example from the woman; despite being the one chosen to bear the Son of God, Mary did not become self-centered and all important. Instead, she called herself lowly, and humbled herself, becoming the first disciple, the first follower of her Son. The evil we encounter in this world, can only be conquered by Christ. And Christ can only work when we put aside our pride, and trust in Him as Mary has done.

August 17, 2008

Twentieth Sunday in Ordinary Time

A reading from the holy Gospel according to Matthew
15:21–28

At that time, Jesus withdrew to the region of Tyre
	and Sidon.
And behold, a Canaanite woman of that district came
	and called out,
	"Have pity on me, Lord, Son of David!
My daughter is tormented by a demon."
But Jesus did not say a word in answer to her.
Jesus' disciples came and asked him,
	"Send her away, for she keeps calling out after us."
He said in reply,
	"I was sent only to the lost sheep of the house
	of Israel."
But the woman came and did Jesus homage, saying,
	"Lord, help me."
He said in reply,
	"It is not right to take the food of the children
	and throw it to the dogs."

She said, "Please, Lord, for even the dogs eat
    the scraps
  that fall from the table of their masters."
Then Jesus said to her in reply,
  "O woman, great is your faith!
Let it be done for you as you wish."
And the woman's daughter was healed from
    that hour.

The Gospel of the Lord.

EXPLANATION OF THE READING

Jesus' words are so atypical that we may fail to see what is actually going
on. It appears that Jesus falls into the standard stereotype, that this woman
was a Canaanite and therefore a dog. In a way, though, Jesus uses the
stereotype against Israel, and really, against us. In this woman we see
genuine humility; how often, though, do we see it in ourselves? Is it not
true that we tend to think of others as less good, less worthy than us?
Jesus uses the prejudices around him as a mirror for us to see ourselves.

August 24, 2008

TWENTY-FIRST SUNDAY IN ORDINARY TIME

A reading from the holy Gospel according to Matthew
16:13–20

Jesus went into the region of Caesarea Philippi and
  he asked his disciples,
  "Who do people say that the Son of Man is?"

They replied, "Some say John the Baptist,
   others Elijah,
  still others Jeremiah or one of the prophets."
He said to them, "But who do you say that I am?"
Simon Peter said in reply,
  "You are the Christ, the Son of the living God."
Jesus said to him in reply,
"Blessed are you, Simon son of Jonah.
For flesh and blood has not revealed this to you,
   but my heavenly Father.
And so I say to you, you are Peter,
  and upon this rock I will build my church,
   and the gates of the netherworld shall not prevail
    against it.
I will give you the keys to the kingdom of heaven.
Whatever you bind on earth shall be bound
   in heaven;
  and whatever you loose on earth shall be loosed
   in heaven."
Then he strictly ordered his disciples
  to tell no one that he was the Christ.

The Gospel of the Lord.

EXPLANATION OF THE READING

Peter's distinctive role among the disciples is attested throughout the Gospel according to Matthew, though he is never idealized; his strong faith and his weaknesses are both vividly depicted. Peter's role is tied firmly to his insight about Jesus' identity as Christ, an identity Jesus insists must remain secret for the moment.

August 31, 2008

Twenty-second Sunday in Ordinary Time

A reading from the holy Gospel according to Matthew

16:21–27

Jesus began to show his disciples
   that he must go to Jerusalem and suffer greatly
   from the elders, the chief priests, and the scribes,
   and be killed and on the third day be raised.
Then Peter took Jesus aside and began to rebuke him,
   "God forbid, Lord! No such thing shall ever
     happen to you."
He turned and said to Peter,
   "Get behind me, Satan! You are an obstacle to me.
You are thinking not as God does, but as human
    beings do."

Then Jesus said to his disciples,
   "Whoever wishes to come after me must
    deny himself,
   take up his cross, and follow me.
For whoever wishes to save his life will lose it,
   but whoever loses his life for my sake will find it.
What profit would there be for one to gain the
    whole world
   and forfeit his life?
Or what can one give in exchange for his life?

For the Son of Man will come with his angels
    in his Father's glory,
    and then he will repay all according to
        his conduct."

The Gospel of the Lord.

EXPLANATION OF THE READING

In trying to find a plausible explanation we do exactly what Peter did;
we try to explain it in human terms. That simply cannot be done. There
is no explanation; the only way we can make sense of the cross is by
accepting it. Even though the cross cannot be defined, it can be seen in
the lives of those who follow Christ. We hear Jesus rebuking Peter: "Get
behind me, Satan!" (Matthew 16:23). And we ask, why Satan? Bishop
Fulton Sheen said that Satan is anyone who opposes the cross. But Christ
accepted the cross, and by doing so we have been saved. The cross
overturns the world.

September 7, 2008

TWENTY-THIRD SUNDAY
IN ORDINARY TIME

A reading from the holy Gospel according to Matthew   18:15-20

Jesus said to his disciples:
"If your brother sins against you,
    go and tell him his fault between you and
        him alone.
If he listens to you, you have won over your brother.
If he does not listen,
    take one or two others along with you,

so that 'every fact may be established
on the testimony of two or three witnesses.'
If he refuses to listen to them, tell the church.
If he refuses to listen even to the church,
then treat him as you would a Gentile or
a tax collector.
Amen, I say to you,
whatever you bind on earth shall be bound
in heaven,
and whatever you loose on earth shall be loosed
in heaven.
Again, amen, I say to you,
if two of you agree on earth
about anything for which they are to pray,
it shall be granted to them by my heavenly Father.
For where two or three are gathered together in
my name,
there am I in the midst of them."

The Gospel of the Lord.

EXPLANATION OF THE READING

The collection of sayings in the selected segment of Gospel according to Matthew describes the qualities and ideal behavior of members of the Church, yesterday and today. It gives practical, fair directives for handling grievances, beginning with one-to-one discussion and gradually calling for the mediation of the community. The step-by-step procedure for dealing with offending members who will not change their ways ends sternly with a kind of excommunication: "Treat him as you would a Gentile or a tax collector" (Matthew 18:17). However, other teachings must be read alongside this one. Throughout the Gospel, Gentiles and sinners are objects of the mission of Jesus. It could be argued that even when banished from the community, erring members are still to be sought out as in the parable of the lost sheep.

September 14, 2008

FEAST OF THE EXALTATION OF THE HOLY CROSS

A reading from the holy Gospel according to John

3:13–17

Jesus said to Nicodemus:
"No one has gone up to heaven
   except the one who has come down from heaven,
      the Son of Man.
And just as Moses lifted up the serpent in the desert,
   so must the Son of Man be lifted up,
      so that everyone who believes in him may have
         eternal life."

For God so loved the world that he gave his only Son,
   so that he who believes in him might not perish
      but might have eternal life.
For God did not send his Son into the world to
      condemn the world,
   but that the world might be saved through him."

The Gospel of the Lord.

EXPLANATION OF THE READING

Today we celebrate the central symbol of Christianity, the cross, an
instrument of torture and cruel death. But for us it is the instrument of
salvation. Lifted up on the cross, Christ broke the power of death and sin,
showed us the Father's love, and we became adopted sons and daughters
of God. The cross is not just a symbol but a way of life. We each have our
share in this mystery. Our willingness to embrace the cross, to give of
ourselves totally, marks us as true followers of Christ.

September 21, 2008

Twenty-fifth Sunday in Ordinary Time

A reading from the holy Gospel according to Matthew

20:1–16a

Jesus told his disciples this parable:
"The kingdom of heaven is like a landowner
  who went out at dawn to hire laborers for
    his vineyard.
After agreeing with them for the usual daily wage,
  he sent them into his vineyard.
Going out about nine o'clock,
  the landowner saw others standing idle in
    the marketplace,
  and he said to them, 'You too go into my vineyard,
  and I will give you what is just.'
So they went off.
And he went out again around noon,
  and around three o'clock, and did likewise.
Going out about five o'clock,
  the landowner found others standing around, and
    said to them,
  'Why do you stand here idle all day?'
They answered, 'Because no one has hired us.'
He said to them, 'You too go into my vineyard.'
When it was evening the owner of the vineyard
    said to his foreman,

'Summon the laborers and give them their pay,
  beginning with the last and ending with the first.'
When those who had started about five o'clock came,
  each received the usual daily wage.
So when the first came, they thought that they would
    receive more,
  but each of them also got the usual wage.
And on receiving it they grumbled against the
    landowner, saying,
  'These last ones worked only one hour,
  and you have made them equal to us,
  who bore the day's burden and the heat.'
He said to one of them in reply,
  'My friend, I am not cheating you.
Did you not agree with me for the usual daily wage?
Take what is yours and go.
What if I wish to give this last one the same as you?
Or am I not free to do as I wish with my own money?
Are you envious because I am generous?'
Thus, the last will be first, and the first will be last."

The Gospel of the Lord.

EXPLANATION OF THE READING

The question of the owner is correct: "Are you envious because I am
generous?" (Matthew 20:15). Envy arises out of our misperception of
justice. When we are envious, we fear that we are not receiving our fair
share. We fail to recognize that everything is a gift. It may be true that
someone is a better singer, but to get envious of her singing talents
means that we fail to see what gifts, what talents we have been given.
And when we spend so much time being envious, we also fail to share
those talents we have been given.

September 28, 2008

Twenty-sixth Sunday in Ordinary Time

A reading from the holy Gospel according to Matthew
21:28–32

Jesus said to the chief priests and elders of
    the people:
"What is your opinion?
A man had two sons.
He came to the first and said,
  'Son, go out and work in the vineyard today.'
He said in reply, 'I will not,'
  but afterwards changed his mind and went.
The man came to the other son and gave the
    same order.
He said in reply, 'Yes, sir,' but did not go.
Which of the two did his father's will?"
They answered, "The first."
Jesus said to them, "Amen, I say to you,
  tax collectors and prostitutes
  are entering the kingdom of God before you.
When John came to you in the way of righteousness,
  you did not believe him;
  but tax collectors and prostitutes did.

Yet even when you saw that,
   you did not later change your minds and
      believe him."

The Gospel of the Lord.

EXPLANATION OF THE READING

Jesus says that "tax collectors and prostitutes are entering the kingdom of God before you." We hear these words and think, "I certainly do not belong to the chief priests and elders, who are hard of heart, and if tax collectors and prostitutes are getting in, then surely I am going to get in, for I am not nearly as bad as they are." But that is where we are the most hard of heart. Where is our love directed? Not to helping the elders and chief priests change their hardened ways, and certainly not in rejoicing that tax collectors and prostitutes have changed their sinful ways. No, our hearts are directed in self congratulations. In this, Christ shows us that we too, have some hardness of heart that needs to be removed.

October 5, 2008

TWENTY-SEVENTH SUNDAY IN ORDINARY TIME

A reading from the holy Gospel according to Matthew   *21:33–43*

Jesus said to the chief priests and the elders of
      the people:
"Hear another parable.
There was a landowner who planted a vineyard,
   put a hedge around it, dug a wine press in it, and
      built a tower.
Then he leased it to tenants and went on a journey.

When vintage time drew near,
    he sent his servants to the tenants to obtain
        his produce.
But the tenants seized the servants and one
        they beat,
    another they killed, and a third they stoned.
Again he sent other servants, more numerous than
        the first ones,
    but they treated them in the same way.
Finally, he sent his son to them, thinking,
    'They will respect my son.'
But when the tenants saw the son, they said to
        one another,
    'This is the heir.
Come, let us kill him and acquire his inheritance.'
They seized him, threw him out of the vineyard, and
        killed him.
What will the owner of the vineyard do to those
        tenants when he comes?"
They answered him,
    "He will put those wretched men to
        a wretched death
    and lease his vineyard to other tenants
    who will give him the produce at the proper times."
Jesus said to them, "Did you never read in
        the Scriptures:
The stone that the builders rejected
    has become the cornerstone;

by the Lord has this been done,
and it is wonderful in our eyes?
Therefore, I say to you,
the kingdom of God will be taken away from you
and given to a people that will produce its fruit."

The Gospel of the Lord.

EXPLANATION OF THE READING

What we do not hear in this parable is what happens once the landlord has new tenants. This time, we presume, he will stay close by. Rather than going on a journey, the landowner will decide to stay as close as possible to the tenants. Indeed, this is the real fruit of the parable; the Lord stays close to us. In fact, he stays so close to us that he gives his very self to us! And he has remained that close ever since, in his Church, in the Eucharist, and in our hearts.

October 12, 2008

TWENTY-EIGHTH SUNDAY IN ORDINARY TIME

A reading from the holy Gospel according to Matthew
22:1–10

Jesus again in reply spoke to the chief priests and
elders of the people
in parables, saying,
"The kingdom of heaven may be likened to a king
who gave a wedding feast for his son.

He dispatched his servants
   to summon the invited guests to the feast,
   but they refused to come.
A second time he sent other servants, saying,
   'Tell those invited: "Behold, I have prepared
      my banquet,
   my calves and fattened cattle are killed,
   and everything is ready; come to the feast."'
Some ignored the invitation and went away,
   one to his farm, another to his business.
The rest laid hold of his servants,
   mistreated them, and killed them.
The king was enraged and sent his troops,
   destroyed those murderers, and burned their city.
Then he said to his servants, 'The feast is ready,
   but those who were invited were not worthy
      to come.
Go out, therefore, into the main roads
   and invite to the feast whomever you find.'
The servants went out into the streets
   and gathered all they found, bad and good alike,
   and the hall was filled with guests.
But when the king came in to meet the guests,
   he saw a man there not dressed in
      a wedding garment.
The king said to him, 'My friend, how is it
   that you came in here without a wedding garment?'
But he was reduced to silence.

Then the king said to his attendants, 'Bind his hands
   and feet,
   and cast him into the darkness outside,
   where there will be wailing and grinding of teeth.'
Many are invited, but few are chosen."

The Gospel of the Lord.

Longer: Matthew 22:1–14

EXPLANATION OF THE READING

How does Jesus' story work on its many audiences? Hearing the
shocking responses of the invited guests—refusals, indifference, and
even murder—we're in sympathy with the outraged host. But then we're
startled by his retaliation. Destroy the murderers? Understandable. Burn
the city? Where is this story headed? The third invitation—to absolutely
everyone—brings in a mixture of "bad and good alike." We're surprised
when, contrary to the usual Christian message about the greater
importance of one's inner state over outer appearance, the host is so
offended by the underdressed guest. "Many are invited, but few are
chosen." What are we to make of it?

October 19, 2008

TWENTY-NINTH SUNDAY
IN ORDINARY TIME

A reading from the holy Gospel
according to Matthew   *22:15–21*

The Pharisees went off
   and plotted how they might entrap Jesus in speech.

They sent their disciples to him, with the Herodians,
saying,
"Teacher, we know that you are a truthful man
and that you teach the way of God in accordance
with the truth.
And you are not concerned with anyone's opinion,
for you do not regard a person's status.
Tell us, then, what is your opinion:
Is it lawful to pay the census tax to Caesar or not?"
Knowing their malice, Jesus said,
"Why are you testing me, you hypocrites?
Show me the coin that pays the census tax."
Then they handed him the Roman coin.
He said to them, "Whose image is this and
whose inscription?"
They replied, "Caesar's."
At that he said to them,
"Then repay to Caesar what belongs to Caesar
and to God what belongs to God."

The Gospel of the Lord.

EXPLANATION OF THE READING

Jesus' teaching addresses the challenge facing faithful people everywhere.
Whether we are paying taxes or paying (with our time, attention, and
money) for things we think are essential, we risk making the government,
products, or the coins themselves the focus of our homage and attention.
So, Jesus recommends, do what is necessary in the world, but don't give
your heart to it. Give to God what belongs to God—all our heart and soul
and mind. Give to God all glory and honor.

October 26, 2008

THIRTIETH SUNDAY IN ORDINARY TIME

A reading from the holy Gospel according to Matthew   22:34–40

When the Pharisees heard that Jesus had silenced
    the Sadducees,
  they gathered together, and one of them,
  a scholar of the law, tested him by asking,
  "Teacher, which comandment in the law is
    the greatest?"
He said to him,
"You shall love the Lord, your God,
  with all your heart,
  with all your soul,
  and with all your mind.
This is the greatest and the first commandment.
The second is like it:
  You shall love your neighbor as yourself.
The whole law and the prophets
    depend on these two commandments."

The Gospel of the Lord.

EXPLANATION OF THE READING

Within the heart of every believer is a stream that murmurs, "Come to
the Father!" and at the same time, "Go to your brother and sister!" This
double flow of love is the perfection of the Law, and in the Eucharist, it
irrigates the city of God, the Church.

November 2, 2008

COMMEMORATION OF ALL THE FAITHFUL DEPARTED (ALL SOULS)

A reading from the holy Gospel according to John
6:37–40

Jesus said to the crowds:

"Everything that the Father gives me will come to me,
    and I will not reject anyone who comes to me,
    because I came down from heaven not to do my
        own will
    but the will of the one who sent me.
And this is the will of the one who sent me,
    that I should not lose anything of what he gave me,
    but that I should raise it on the last day.
For this is the will of my Father,
    that everyone who sees the Son and believes in him
    may have eternal life,
    and I shall raise him on the last day."

The Gospel of the Lord.

Note: Other Gospels for this day can be found in the Lectionary.

EXPLANATION OF THE READING

In this time of shorter days and colder nights we stop to remember our grandparents, or maybe a sister or brother, a mother or father, our friends and neighbors, all the faithful who have departed. We pray that they may inherit the promise that Christ has offered. For we know that no one reaches perfection while in this life, but Christ will not reject anyone who comes to him. We pray that in the flames of purgatory the person shall not be harmed but made perfect by the work of God. We pray that the heart of the faithful shall be consumed with the love and joy of God, as he draws that person to himself. In this dark time of the year, as the year approaches its end, we stop to give thanks, for a life that has touched us, for a love that was shown to us, and for a promise that was given to us.

November 9, 2008

FEAST OF THE DEDICATION OF THE LATERAN BASILICA IN ROME

A reading from the holy Gospel according to John

2:13–22

Since the Passover of the Jews was near,
   Jesus went up to Jerusalem.
He found in the temple area those who sold oxen,
      sheep, and doves,
   as well as the money changers seated there.
He made a whip out of cords
   and drove them all out of the temple area,
      with the sheep and oxen,
   and spilled the coins of the money changers
   and overturned their tables,
   and to those who sold doves he said,
   "Take these out of here,
   and stop making my Father's house
      a marketplace."
His disciples recalled the words of Scripture,
   Zeal for your house will consume me.
At this the Jews answered and said to him,
   "What sign can you show us for doing this?"

Jesus answered and said to them,

"Destroy this temple and in three days I will raise
it up."

The Jews said,

"This temple has been under construction for
forty-six years,

and you will raise it up in three days?"

But he was speaking about the temple of his Body.

Therefore, when he was raised from the dead,

his disciples remembered that he had said this,

and they came to believe the Scripture

and the word Jesus had spoken.

The Gospel of the Lord.

EXPLANATION OF THE READING

The Temple, the basilica, the church, are all places of prayer; holy sites
where we encounter God in a most profound way. But St. Paul reminds us
that God also dwells within us. "Do you not know that you are the temple
of God and that the Spirit of God dwells in you?" (1 Corinthians 3:16).
Maybe, then, the cleaning of the Temple is a message. Maybe we are the
ones who need to be cleaned up. What things are in us, what thoughts or
actions have we done that do not belong in the Temple of the Lord? What
images have we allowed into our minds and hearts? What jealousies or
hatreds have we maintained? What lust or greed have we permitted to
stay in the very place where God wants to be?

November 16, 2008

THIRTY-THIRD SUNDAY IN ORDINARY TIME

A reading from the holy Gospel according to Matthew   *25:14–30*

Jesus told his disciples this parable:
"A man going on a journey
    called in his servants and entrusted his possessions
        to them.
To one he gave five talents; to another, two;
        to a third, one—
    to each according to his ability.
Then he went away.
Immediately the one who received five talents
        went and traded with them,
    and made another five.
Likewise, the one who received two made
        another two.
But the man who received one went off and dug
        a hole in the ground
    and buried his master's money.

"After a long time
    the master of those servants came back
    and settled accounts with them.
The one who had received five talents came forward
    bringing the additional five.

He said, 'Master, you gave me five talents.
See, I have made five more.'
His master said to him, 'Well done, my good and
    faithful servant.
Since you were faithful in small matters,
  I will give you great responsibilities.
Come, share your master's joy.'
Then the one who had received two talents also
    came forward and said,
  'Master, you gave me two talents.
See, I have made two more.'
His master said to him, 'Well done, my good and
    faithful servant.
Since you were faithful in small matters,
  I will give you great responsibilities.
Come, share your master's joy.'
Then the one who had received the one talent came
    forward and said,
  'Master, I knew you were a demanding person,
  harvesting where you did not plant
  and gathering where you did not scatter;
  so out of fear I went off and buried your talent in
    the ground.
Here it is back.'
His master said to him in reply, 'You wicked,
    lazy servant!
So you knew that I harvest where I did not plant
  and gather where I did not scatter?

Should you not then have put my money in the bank
   so that I could have got it back with interest on
      my return?
Now then! Take the talent from him and give it to
      the one with ten.
For to everyone who has,
   more will be given and he will grow rich;
   but from the one who has not,
   even what he has will be taken away.
And throw this useless servant into the
      darkness outside,
   where there will be wailing and grinding of teeth.'"

The Gospel of the Lord.

Shorter: Matthew 25:14–15, 19–21

EXPLANATION OF THE READING

We understand how we have been given gifts from God, gifts that we are
to use. Is it not then troubling that God, the master of the place, is so
demanding in this parable? It is all the more so when we hear it now,
toward the end of the liturgical year, when we hear of the end times. The
talents that we receive, even more than as gifts, can be understood as our
ability to love. And so we must remember to be vigilant in how we love,
and the end times will bring no fear.

November 23, 2008

Solemnity of Our Lord Jesus Christ the King/Last Week in Ordinary Time

A reading from the holy Gospel according to Matthew   *25:31–46*

Jesus said to his disciples:
"When the Son of Man comes in his glory,
    and all the angels with him,
    he will sit upon his glorious throne,
    and all the nations will be assembled before him.
And he will separate them one from another,
    as a shepherd separates the sheep from the goats.
He will place the sheep on his right and the goats on
        his left.
Then the king will say to those on his right,
    'Come, you who are blessed by my Father.
Inherit the kingdom prepared for you
        from the foundation of the world.
For I was hungry and you gave me food,
    I was thirsty and you gave me drink,
    a stranger and you welcomed me,
    naked and you clothed me,
    ill and you cared for me,
    in prison and you visited me.'

Then the righteous will answer him and say,
'Lord, when did we see you hungry and feed you,
or thirsty and give you drink?
When did we see you a stranger and welcome you,
or naked and clothe you?
When did we see you ill or in prison, and visit you?'
And the king will say to them in reply,
'Amen, I say to you, whatever you did
for one of the least brothers of mine, you did
for me.'
Then he will say to those on his left,
'Depart from me, you accursed,
into the eternal fire prepared for the devil and
his angels.
For I was hungry and you gave me no food,
I was thirsty and you gave me no drink,
a stranger and you gave me no welcome,
naked and you gave me no clothing,
ill and in prison, and you did not care for me.'
Then they will answer and say,
'Lord, when did we see you hungry or thirsty
or a stranger or naked or ill or in prison,
and not minister to your needs?'
He will answer them, 'Amen, I say to you,
what you did not do for one of these least ones,
you did not do for me.'
And these will go off to eternal punishment,
but the righteous to eternal life."

The Gospel of the Lord.

EXPLANATION OF THE READING

If you have never been lost, never known anguish, if you have never been wounded or found weak, then you are far from experiencing the kingship of Jesus Christ. If, on the contrary, you know yourself as wounded, broken, and restless, then rejoice and be glad, for the kingdom of Christ is very near to you. He waits to place at your service all the kingly resources of his merciful love.

Patron Saints

The saints and blesseds are our companions in prayer on our journey with Christ. Here we provide you with a list of health concerns and the saints chosen to intercede on a sick person's behalf before God the Father.

AILMENTS	SAINT(S)
A	
abdominal pains	Agapitus; Charles Borromeo; Emerentiana; Erasmus; Liborius
abortion, protection against	Catherine of Sweden
abuse victims	Adelaide; Agostina Pietrantoni; Fabiola; John Baptist de la Salle; Germaine Cousin; Godelieve; Jeanne de Lestonnac; Jeanne Marie de Maille; Joaquina Vedruna de Mas; Laura Vicuna; Margaret the Barefooted; Maria Bagnesi; Monica; Pharaildis; Rita of Cascia
AIDS patients	Aloysius Gonzaga; Therese of Lisieux; Peregrine Lazios
alcoholism	John of God; Martin of Tours; Matthias the Apostle; Monica; Urban of Langres
angina sufferers	Swithbert
appendicitis	Erasmus (Elmo)
apoplexy, apoplexies, stroke, stroke victims	Andrew Avellino; Wolfgang
arm pain; pain in the arms	Amalburga

B

babies	The Holy Innocents; Maximus; Nicholas of Tolentino; Philip of Zell
bacterial disease and infection	Agrippina
barren women	Anthony of Padua; Felicity
barrenness, against	Agatha; Anne; Anthony of Padua; Casilda of Toledo; Felicity; Fiacre; Francis of Paola; Giles; Henry II; Margaret of Antioch; Medard; Philomena; Rita of Cascia; Theobald Roggeri
birth complications, against	Ulric
birth pains	Erasmus
blind people, blindness	Catald; Cosmas and Damian; Dunstan; Lawrence the Illuminator; Leodegarius; Lucy; Lutgardis; Odila; Parasceva; Raphael the Archangel; Thomas the Apostle
blood donors	Our Lady of the Thorns
bodily ills, illness, sickness	Alphais; Alphonsa of India; Angela Merici; Angela Truszkowska; Arthelais; Bathild; Bernadette of Lourdes; Camillus of Lellis; Catherine del Ricci; Catherine of Siena; Drogo; Edel Quinn; Elizabeth of the Trinity; Gerard of Villamagna; Germaine Cousin; Gorgonia; Hugh of Lincoln; Isabella of France; Jacinta Marto; John of God; Julia Billiart; Julia Falconieri; Juliana of Nicomedia; Louis IX; Louise de Marillac; Lydwina of Schiedam; Maria Bagnesi; Maria Gabriella; Maria Mazzarello; Marie Rose Durocher; Mary Ann de Paredes; Mary Magdalen of Pazzi; Michael the

Archangel; Our Lady of Lourdes; Paula
Frassinetti; Peregrine Laziosi; Philomena;
Rafka Al-Rayes; Raphael; Romula;
Syncletica; Teresa of Avila; Teresa Valse
Pantellini; Terese of the Andes; Therese
of Lisieux

breast cancer	Agatha; Aldegundis; Giles; Peregrine
breast disease, against	Agatha
breastfeeding women	Giles
broken bones	Drogo; Stanislaus Kostka

C

cancer patients; against cancer	Aldegundis; Giles; James Salomone; Peregrine Laziosi
child abuse victims	Alodia; Germaine Cousin; Lufthild; Nunilo
childbirth	Erasmus; Gerard Majella; Leonard of Noblac; Lutgardis; Margaret (or Marina) of Antioch; Raymond Nonnatus
childhood diseases	Aldegundis; Pharaildis
childhood intestinal diseases	Erasmus
children, convulsive	Guy of Anderlecht; John the Baptist; Scholastica
children, death of	Alphonsa Hawthorne; Angela of Foligno; Clotilde; Conception Cabrera de Annida; Cyriacus of Iconium; Dorothy of Montau; Elizabeth of Hungary; Elizabeth Ann Seton; Felicity; Frances of Rome; Hedwig; Isidore the Farmer; Joaquina Vedruna de Mas; Julitta; Leopold the Good; Louis IX; Luchesius; Margaret of Scotland; Marguerite d'Youville; Matilda; Melania the Younger;

	Michelina; Nonna; Perpetua; Stephen of Hungary
children, sick	Beuno; Clement I; Hugh of Lincoln; Ubaldus Baldassini
children, stammering	Notkar Balbulus
colic	Agapitus; Charles Borremo; Emerentiana; Erasmus; Liborius
contagious diseases	Robert Bellarmine; Sebastian
consumption	Pantaleon; Therese of Liseux
convulsions	John the Baptist; Willibrord
coughs, against	Blaise; Quentin; Walburga
cramps, against	Cadoc of Llancarvan; Maurice; Pancras
cures from pain	Madron

D

deaf people, deafness	Cadoc of Llancarvan; Drogo; Francis de Sales; Meriadoc; Ouen
death	Michael the Archangel; Margaret (or Marina) of Antioch
death, happy	Joseph; Ulric
death, against sudden	Aldegundis; Andrew Avellino; Barbara; Christopher
disabled, handicapped	Alphais; Angela Merici; Gerald of Aurillac; Germaine Cousin; Giles; Henry II; Lutgardis; Margaret of Castello; Seraphina; Servatus; Servulus
drug abuse	Maximillian Kolbe
dying people, invoked by	Abel; Barbara; Benedict; Catherine of Alexandria; James the Lesser, Apostle; John of God; Joseph; Margaret (or

Marina) of Antioch; Michael the
Archangel; Nicholas of Tolentino;
Sebastian

dysentary	Lucy of Syracuse; Polycarp

E

earache, against	Cornelius; Polycarp of Smyrna
epidemics	Godeberta; Lucy of Syracuse; Our Lady of Zapopan; Roch (Rocco)
epilepsy, epileptics	Alban of Mainz; Anthony the Abbot; Balthasar; Bibiana; Catald; Christopher; Cornelius; Dymphna; Genesius; Gerard of Lunel; Giles; Guy of Anderlecht; John Chrysostom; John the Baptist; Valentine; Vitus; Willibrord
ergotism, aginst	Anthony the Abbot
erysipelas	Anthony the Abbot; Benedict; Ida of Nivelles
expectant Mothers	Gerard Majella; Raymond Nonnatus
eyes, eye diseases, eye problems, sore eyes	Aloysius Gonzaga; Augustine of Hippo; Clare of Assisi; Cyriacus of Iconium; Erhard of Regensburg; Herve; Leodegarius; Lucy of Syracuse; Raphael the Archangel; Symphorian of Autun

F

fainting, faintness	Urban of Langres; Ursus of Ravenna; Valentine
fever, against	Abraham; Adalard; Amalberga; Andrew Abellon; Antoninus of Florence; Benedict; Castorus; Claudius; Cornelius; Dominic of Sora; Domitian of Huy; Four

Crowned Martyrs; Genevieve;
Gerebernus; Gertrude of Nivelles; Hugh
of Cluny; Jodocus; Liborius; Mary of
Oignies; Nicostratus; Peter the Apostle;
Petronilla; Raymond Nonnatus; Severus
of Avranches; Sigismund; Simpronian;
Theobald Roggeri; Ulric; Winnoc

fistula	Fiacre
frenzy, against	Denis; Peter the Apostle; Ulric
foot problems; feet problems	Peter the Apostle; Servatus

G

gall stones	Benedict; Drogo; Florentius of Strasburg; Liborius
goiter	Blaise
gout, against; gout sufferers	Andrew the Apostle; Coloman; Gerebernus; Gregory the Great; Killian; Maurice; Maurus; Totman

H

hangovers	Bibiana
head injuries	John Licci
headaches	Acacius; Anastasius the Persian; Bibiana; Denis; Dionysius the Aeropagite; Gerard of Lunel; Gereon; Pancras; Stephen the Martyr; Teresa of Avila; William Firmatus
health	Infant Jesus of Prague
healthy throats	Andrew the Apostle; Blaise; Etheldreda; Godelieve; Ignatius of Antioch; Lucy of Syracuse; Swithbert
heart patients	John of God
hemorrhage	Lucy

hemorrhoid, piles	Fiacre
hernia	Alban of Mainz; Condrad Piacenzai; Cosmas and Damian; Drogo; Gummarus
herpes	George
hoarseness, against	Bernadine of Sienna; Maurus
hydrophobia (rabies)	Dominic de Silos; Guy of Anderlecht; Hubert of Liege; Otto of Bamberg; Sithney; Walburga

I

infertility, against	Agatha; Anne; Anthony of Padua; Casilda of Toledo; Felicity; Fiacre; Francis of Paola; Giles; Henry II; Margaret of Antioch; Medard; Philomena; Rita of Cascia; Theobald Roggeri
inflammatory disease	Benedict
intestinal diseases, against	Brice; Charles Borromeo; Emerentiana; Erasmus; Timonthy; Wolfgang
invalids, homebound	Roch (Rocco)

J

jauntice	Odilo

K

kidney disease, against	Benedict; Drogo; Margaret (or Marina) of Antioch; Ursus of Ravenna
kidney stones; gravel	Alban of Mainz
knee diseases or trouble	Roch (Rocco)

L

lame, the	Giles
leg diseases, leg trouble	Servatus

lepers, leprosy	George; Giles; Lazarus; Vincent de Paul
long life	Peter the Apostle
lumbago	Lawrence

M

mental illness	Benedict Joseph Labre; Bibiana; Christina the Astonishing; Drogo; Dymphna; Eustochium of Padua; Fillan; Giles; Job; Margaret of Cortona; Maria Fortunata Viti; Medard; Michelina; Osmund; Raphaela; Romanus of Condat; Veran
migraine	Gereon; Severus of Avranches; Ulbadus Baldassini
milk, loss of by nursing women	Margaret of Antioch
miscarriage, against	Catherine of Sienna; Catherine of Sweden; Eulalia
miscarriage prevention	Catherine of Sweeden
muteness	Drogo

N

near sightedness, short sightedness	Clarus; Abbot
nerve or neurological disease, against	Bartholomew the Apostle; Dymphna
nursing mothers	Concordia; Martina

O

obsession	Quirinus

P

pain relief	Madron
paralysis	Catald; Osmund; Wolfgang

physical spouse abuse, against; victims of spouse abuse, against	Rita of Cascia
plague, against	Adrian of Nicomedia; Catald; Colman of Stockerau; Cuthbert; Edmund of East Anglia; Erhard of Regensburg; Francis of Paola; Francis Xavier; George; Genevieve; Gregory the Great; Macarius of Antioch; Roch (Rocco); Sebastian; Valentine; Walburga
poison sufferers	Benedict; Abbot; John the Apostles; Pirmin
pregnant women, pregnancy	Anne; Anthony of Padua; Elizabeth; Gerard Majella; Joseph; Margaret (or Marina) of Antioch; Raymond Nonnatus; Ulric

R

rape victims	Agatha; Agnes of Rome; Antona Messina; Dymphna; Joan of Arc; Maria Goretti; Pierina Morosini; Potamiaena; Solange; Zita
rheumatism, arthritis	Alphonus Maria de Liguori; Coloman; James the Greater; Killian; Servatus; Totnan
respiratory problems	Bernadine of Sienna
ruptures, against	Drogo; Florentius of Strasburg; Osmund

S

scrofulous diseases	Balbina; Marculf; Mark the Evangelist
skin disease	Anthony the Abbot; George; Marculf; Peregrine Laziosi; Roch (Rocco)
skin rashes	Anthony the Abbot; George; Marculf; Peregrine Laziosi; Roch (Rocco)

sleepwalkers, sleepwalking	Dymphna
smallpox	Matthias
snakebite victims	Hilary; Paul
spasms	John the Baptist
sterility, against	Agatha; Anne; Anthony of Padua; Casilda of Toledo; Felicity; Fiacre; Francis of Paola; Giles; Henry II; Margaret of Antioch; Medard; Philomena; Rita of Cascia; Theobald Roggeri
stillborn children	Edmund
stomach disease, stomach trouble	Brice; Charles Borromeo; Erasmus; Timothy; Wolfgang
stroke	Andrew Avellino; Wolfgang
struma	Balbina; Marculf; Mark the Evangelist
surgery patients	Infant of Prague
syphilis	Fiacre; George; Symphoroian of Autun

T

throat diseases, against	Andrew the Apostle; Blaise; Etheldreda; Godelieve; Ignatius of Antioch; Lucy of Syracuse; Swithbert
toothaches	Apollonia; Chirstopher; Elizabeth of Hungary; Ida of Nivelles; Kea; Medard; Osmund
tuberculosis	Pantaleon; Theresa of Liseaux
twitching, against	Bartholomew the Apostle; Cornelius
typhus, against; against typhoid	Adelard

u

ulcers, against	Charles Borromeo; Job

V

venereal disease	Fiacre
verbal spousal abuse	Anne Marie Taigi; Godelieve; Monica
vertigo, against	Ulric

W

whooping cough, against	Blaise; Winoc
women in labor	Anne; Erasmus; John of Bridlington; Margaret (or Marina) of Antioch; Margaret of Fontana; Mary of Oignies
women who wish to be mothers	Andrew the Apostle
wounds	Aldegundis; Marciana; Rita of Cascia

NOTES

NOTES

NOTES

Handbook for Ministers of Care

Paperback, 6 x 9, 96 pages
978-1-56854-102-0
Order code: HBMCR2 **$8**

GENEVIEVE GLEN, OSB, MARILYN KOFLER, SP, AND KEVIN E. O'CONNOR ■ This is a manual for those already involved in the ministry of care, and for those preparing to undertake this vital work. In these pages you will learn a theology of sickness and suffering, how the Communion ritual works, practical advice on making pastoral visits, how to take care of yourself while caring for others, and where to find further information about illnesses affecting those you visit.

AWARDS:

Catholic Press Association 1998 Book Award winner, first place, in pastoral ministry

8IANV7

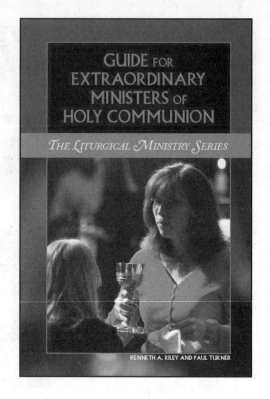